CLAIRE'S DAD

CLAIRE'S DAD

How I Earned the Title

Grow Your Relationship with Your Daughter Through Persuasive
and Challenging Insights, Practical Tools, and Encouraging Stories
that Will Inspire You to Earn the Title of DAD

Shad Arnold

Edited by
Claire E. Arnold and G. F. Boyer

ISBN: 0692992774
ISBN 13: 9780692992777
Library of Congress Control Number: 2017962823
Pinpoint Innovation, Inc., Orange, CA

Bible references are from the NIV (New International Version), Copyright 1986 by Holman Bible Publishers; The Holy Bible, New International Version, Copyright 1973, 1978, 1984 by the International Bible Society; and New King James Version®, Copyright © 1982 by Thomas Nelson.

Into the Fire, lyrics by Nan Knighton and music by Frank Wildhorn © 1992, 1998 WB Music Corp. Knight Errant Music, Scaramanga Music, and Bronx Flash Music, Inc. Referenced video performance performed on the album and video of *Stand Ye Steady: Songs of Courage and Inspiration*, performed by Daniel Rodriguez and the USMA Cadet Glee Club. © Curtain Call Productions, LLC.

I dedicate this book to every father who strives to be a loving, faithful, and honest father to his children. Be the tenacious defender of your family from all that comes against it. Be an example for your daughter to follow and your son to emulate. Do what it takes to *earn* the title of Dad. Hold fast! Never give up!

And...

To Janelle, my wife, best friend, business and life partner, and outstanding mother to Claire and Blake. You are the key to any success I have had or will ever know. As it happens, this book is so finely tuned and hyper focused on the role as a dad and my journey therein that a casual reader may read on without measurable consideration of you and all that you have done for our family, our children, and our lives together. It would be incomplete to our collective story, and certainly unjust to the broader composition of our family, to imagine the journey without your input, care, and depth. The simple and undisputed facts are that, without your support, advice, and heart, I may not have earned the title and our family would not be what it is today. There is no *Dad* in this family apart from *Mom*; there is no *Shad* without *Janelle*.

All my love and respect are yours.

—Shad
January 2018

Contents

Introduction: How and Why This Book Came to Be

Men are inherently logical and action-oriented creatures. The problem comes when we become creatures of habit and rely solely on logic and action to get us through "the dad years." Sounds right...right? Wrong. Our daughters, their needs and—yes, dare I say it—their emotions are not always logical. Additionally, there is no such span of time that you can refer to as the "dad years" (unless, of course, you acknowledge that it begins with conception and ends when one or the other passes away). You will *always* be in the dad years; however, you will likely have the greatest influence on your daughter during the years she is at home.

Consider how you would use logic and action upon receipt of a standard letter-size envelope in the mail. After retrieving a letter from the mailbox, you notice the envelope in question is addressed to you. You have been awaiting its delivery—though the contents are not completely known to you—and you *know* you want to open it. Do you tear it open, eviscerating the once neatly folded and sealed pouch? Do you wait until you can locate a letter opener? Do you carefully release the seal with your finger as you slowly insert your index finger into the corner of the flap and progress ever so gently until the envelope opens completely? Do you tear the end open and pluck out the contents like a surgeon?

There is no right or wrong answer. The point is that your logic, action, and reaction are only a small part of what will help you be a great dad to your daughter. You need more along the way, because your daughter is no standard letter-size envelope. Your daughter is a very delicate soul who must be carried and cared for with special attention.

Daughters are a unique species. "Species?" you ask. Well, what else would you call them? They are so very unique and set apart from sons. They are a gift from God; they come in many colors, shapes, and sizes, but they are all unique—a species unto themselves.

They have ingrained thoughts, feelings, and emotional responses to their fathers, and that is why we sometimes miss the mark and don't know what to say, how to respond, or when to do either. They are different. They are special. They are our daughters.

This book is not a magic pill or proven game plan for successful relationships and growth; nor is it to be considered something to be implemented to the exclusion of your son(s). It is a collection of thoughts; excerpts from my life with my daughter, Claire; records of hits and misses; and an open heart for you to explore and grow in your journey—another tool in your toolbox. It is my hope and prayer that you are a part of building something—someone—great with it: your daughter.

As you read on, stop at each of the chapter conclusions to reference the chapter recap and checklist. Remind yourself of each point that was carefully considered in the chapter, and take a moment to put a check in each box. Each box and the subsequent check you place in it will confirm the points raised and your desire to see it through, to act on it, or to simply acknowledge it and move forward.

This is a humble book that *had* to be written, in part because so many people supported its development, celebrated its importance, and asked for it. But more than that, this book must be *read*, because so many fathers need to develop and implement their title role as dad.

As fathers, we are generally unprepared, untrained, and unwilling (if we're honest) to change or adapt too much in order to understand and grow with things that we don't see logic in. That is just how we are built— but that is *not* how your daughter was created.

Take a minute to consider your daughter's uniqueness. Think of these descriptors as you begin the journey, that is, this humble book.

Your daughter is sole, single, exclusive, exceptional, inimitable, distinctive, matchless, irreplaceable, rare, and one of a kind, and she is *yours*!

She's worth a few hours of reading. And who knows—you may enjoy and grow in a few areas along the way.

Time: Your First Gift to Her

Lamaze classes, executive-level planning sessions (because I am a type-A man and a planner), assembling baby furniture, painting, investing in diapers by the caseload, choosing a name, and more could not have prepared me for this. The moment was here. She was coming, and nothing was going to stop it now. Hours of labor, breathing, encouragement, pushing, and sweating literally delivered our first child: my daughter, my love, the precious and irreplaceable gift from God.

She was here. Tears of joy, shock, and trepidation came quickly. I was now a dad, and the experiences we would have together would lead me to write this book. Our lessons and adventures boarded an outbound train in time that would take us through seasons of change and challenge, storms and sunshine. I discovered along the way, within the fog of "life," awaiting quiet reflection—or decidedly sweet confirmation—that she had grown up, and through determined effort and a lot of mistakes, I had earned the title "Dad."

That is how it goes. Decades later, I am reminded of the moments, the times, and the travails. What did I learn? How did we survive? Why did we do it the way we did?

If you're a dad or about to become one, this book is for you. Written for you, it is a tool in your toolbox in your work to create balanced, secure, loving growth of *your* gift, *your* investment, *your* daughter.

Similar to any number of tools you'd find in a toolbox, this exposé, this unvarnished and open letter in book form that I've written to you, has some rough edges. You may find this tool hard to grasp or find it to be an uncomfortable fit in your hands. You may, however, discover that it's the unpolished, not-so-smooth, and stippled finish of the tool that is exactly what you need. Exposed within are the hard realities of a dad who won and lost his battle along the way, but who walked with his daughter through it all and earned the title.

The challenge—your challenge—is to board the train, to learn from the challenges, and to be your daughter's dad. Don't just claim the title. Earn it.

I write this on a day when I am actually considering how fast the time has passed. For those of you who read this and are about to become a father or those of you who are in the midst of diapers, car seats, and strollers, remember this: it will pass—and all too quickly!

We've heard it said throughout our lives: "Time passes by so fast," "Those kids will grow up before your eyes, and you'll wonder where the years went," and "Hold them close while they're young; they'll be grown up and gone before you know it." These seemingly cliché statements are real. They are hard to fully grasp while you're in the moment, but they are nevertheless true. Hold fast!

As I type these words, I am sitting in my home office looking at one of my favorite pictures that I keep on my desk: a photo of my son, Blake, with my daughter, Claire, on her first day of kindergarten, standing together on our porch, with her arm over his shoulders, and his nearly three-years-younger little hands grasping her fingers tightly.

Smiles abound, and yes, it is a sweet photo. But what is not seen in this picture are the tears that Blake cried over his big sister's departure. Kindergarten was only a few hours a day, but to him it was forever. To him, it was painful—genuinely painful. Why? He loved her so deeply. He cherished the time with her. He felt her happiness and sadness equally.

Blake was (and still is) the quintessential empathetic human being. From the age of two through perhaps seven years of age, if Claire was disciplined—which happened quite often in her early years, I might add—he would cry. His tears were as heartfelt and genuine as if he had been put in time-out or received a spanking himself. It got to the point that Janelle and I began to consider where he was when we would punish her so that, if possible, he would not know she was being disciplined. Wow, those were the days.

One time, even though I knew the answer to the question, I asked him, "Why are you crying, Blake? You're not in trouble—Claire is."

He looked at me with tear-swollen eyes and said, "I know, Daddy, but I'm sad. Claire's in trouble."

Later as he grew older, he would walk out of the room so that we could not see his tears. Sometimes, finding him sitting on his bed (as if he had been placed in time-out) with silent tears running down his cheeks, we would ask, "Blake, are you all right?" He would silently nod his head to feign a maturity and control over his emotions he did not yet possess. He would then quickly tighten his lips and look away to pick up a toy or some other distraction so that we wouldn't know he was crying over her.

So, other than a God-given empathetic heart for others (in this case for his big sister), what would impart in Blake such a deep connection to his sister and her pain? I submit to you that it is time. They were like twins in some ways—regardless of the age difference—always doing, experiencing, and growing together. Time.

As your daughter's daddy, your first and most profound gift is time. You may pause and think the contrary: it is love. But without time invested, how would she ever know and truly experience your love? She needs your time. You need that same time. Always doing, experiencing, and growing together. Time.

CAREER, TRAVEL, TIME

This is an area that I recognize could immediately turn many readers off, but it must be said. I hope you receive these words in consideration of your daughter and not let ego enter it.

From birth to age eighteen, I believe in my heart that it is imperative that you limit your travel and time away from your family. I cannot begin to know or attempt to address your specific family and career goals and issues, but from personal experience and the unfortunate experience of colleagues in and out of my profession whose crumbling or devastated relationships I have witnessed, the fact is clear. Daughters do not thrive and bond with their fathers when their fathers are gone. Sadly, this fact is observable in too many families today. Too many daughters seek love, attention, and time from unsavory elements found in schools, society, or in the morass of the Internet when there is not a father close at hand.

So, before you may counter with any number of reasons, compelling arguments, or cop-outs as to why your time with your daughter is limited, hear me out. I don't know what your responsibilities are professionally or what is expected of you in your position or what may be expected of you along your career path. I *do* know what I did to mitigate these issues and that you would do well to consider what you can do too.

While my daughter was home for eighteen years, I traveled on business and for volunteer work to forty-nine of the fifty states and to seventeen countries, so I know where some of you are coming from. Travel for many of us is a necessity, but there are ways you can mitigate and redirect the compelled time away.

During most of Claire's time at home, I held sales-management positions within the lighting industry, and I later launched my own businesses in the same field and beyond. In the lighting industry, as in many others, there are any number of high-paying, great-benefit, prestigious positions to aspire to that happen to include extensive travel and often relocation. I never pursued any of them, although I desired all their "benefits." I chose instead to remain in one territory within Southern California to limit my required travel and to ensure that I was home every night for my family. Of course, "every night" is impossible, but the thrust of my family focus and the core belief in what needed to be done were clear to me.

Therefore, I opted for positions that would primarily keep me local. With a few exceptions, my client interactions, entertainment, and events with them took place within forty miles of my home. Even when client meetings stretched into the late afternoon, I would very rarely offer—or accept—an invitation to extend our time together into the dinner hours or beyond. Client and sales interactions never included bars, clubs, or other establishments that I would not want my wife or daughter to be in. My clients needed to know, along with my wife and kids, that my priorities were at home. Additionally, when I was *not* at home, I acted the same way and went to the same places where I would go while with them. Too many men in sales and other "on-the-road" jobs lose their focus and begin to play a game of two men—the one at work and the one at home. Instead, be the same good man. The same good husband. The same great dad.

Yes, I have felt the sting of more than a few snide comments and taken it on the chin over nearly thirty years. I do believe that my career took a financial hit that some in the same position would not be willing to accept; however, it was the right decision. We never went hungry, nor were we ever truly in need. God's provision and my determination to actually have an abundant family life above my career worked out quite well, and I would change very little about it.

In fact, the one change that does come to mind is the knowledge—and embarrassment—that during a period in my life and career while working toward a partnership, I actually worked too much and gave an excessive amount of my family time away to the company, to its success, and I took my eye off the prize. I split my time, talent, and emotional energy for a time, all in the name of "providing for my family." This is one of many lessons learned along the journey of being a father, husband, and career-minded man.

Other limitations that are especially hard to overcome and mitigate (such as divorce, work schedules and conflicts, and others) are valid, but they can be lessened with calculated effort. Men, this is simply a challenge to you now so that you won't regret it later. Make the effort to commit the time.

It has been said that when you're on your deathbed, you'll never wish you'd spent more time at work. You'll wish you'd spent more time with your family. Life is full of regrets. Don't make this one of them.

TEATIME, READING, HOMEWORK, AND MUSICALS

Making time for your daughter (even with homework) demonstrates your love and commitment to her like nothing else, but what do you do with that time? Some of you, for reasons stated or unstated here, will have limited and cherished time with her. So what do you do? This of course varies to a large degree, depending upon her age and temperament, but if you're starting young (which you should, if possible), simple and focused time is better. She will ultimately respond and remember the deep one-on-one time periods over flashy gifts, trips to amusement parks, and the like.

In my experience, one of Claire's favorite things was to have tea together at her little dolly table-and-chair set she had set up in her room for a time. For me, it was utterly painful—both physically and mentally. I did not possess the body frame or spinal fortitude to enjoy the seating arrangements, and I had a difficult time playing to the moment and what the role required. But I did it. To this day, she remembers the teatimes, and although it only happened a few times by comparison to our other adventures, it was well worth it—for both of us.

Reading to her and with her—and eventually having her read to you—is important. Some of my fondest recollections are actually when I would read to Claire. I would read children's books with her on the couch while she was cuddled up next to me. As she stared intently at the pictures, I would read with a different accent for each character, exaggerating my tone and inflection. When she was old enough to appreciate Bible stories, I would do the same. She loved it. In fact, she adored it, and it was something that became a cherished time for Claire—and later with both of my kids. Looking back, we only have a single video clip of one of the storytime moments with the kids, and I am thankful to Janelle for sneaking into the living room to record it. It is a precious memory that is immortalized in video, with both Claire and Blake giggling as I read. It is special. Men, endeavor to make precious memories like that.

To be honest, reading those stories—and even making up a few on the fly—made the close, one-on-one time when I was supposed to be "dad" bearable for me. I did not grow up that way, so it was not a learned experience or a response to that same sort of time invested by *my* dad. It was a decision I made to bond and spend time with her, which took some doing in my heart and psyche. Maybe for you it won't, but if it does, do it anyway.

As Claire grew older, our "daddy/daughter dates"—which I will discuss at length in chapter 3—matured, and we went to musicals together. Now some of you might be experiencing a stage-one or two panic attack right now at the mere thought of this, but this is one of those "dig deep" moments, and it's something I guarantee you will not regret.

Depending upon her age, start with simple stuff like cartoon or movie characters on ice skates if that fits her age and temperament, but don't limit yourself to that. Move on to the classics like *My Fair Lady*, *The King and I*, and *Singing in the Rain*, among others. Then you can progress into modern hits like *Phantom of the Opera*. If you're like me and you enjoy these anyway, great. If you are one of those who is still panting, sweating, or twitching at the thought of it, get over it (and yourself) and buy the tickets. This will be one of the greatest experiences the two of you will look back on with joy. And remember, it should be *dinner and a show*, so there is an upside to it for you: there's food involved (and you can order a dessert for you two to share).

Aside from these examples, learn to develop an interest in what interests her. She may have an interest in an area that you do not have interest in. Dig in. Find out what makes her tick, and develop an interest with her. If you are a sports nut, don't assume that she will be (or should be) and take her to a game and consider it good. Get to know her, and treat the time with her as a valuable commodity, a time capsule that will someday be opened in your minds and hearts. When she is older and opens it in her heart and reminisces, she won't recall silly details; she will only remember that you invested in her and in something she was interested in.

When Claire was small, it was all about "Elmo's World." She loved it, so I became an aficionado of all things Elmo. I could sing the song (and sound like him) and make her Elmo doll dance around like him at the same time. Yes, it felt silly, and I didn't brag about it at work, but Claire loved it, giggled incessantly, and begged for more. Full disclosure: I loathed Elmo. Like most kid characters out there, I grew tired and annoyed of them quickly, and I would often remove myself from the nonstop video play of the show and go mow the lawn or something. But for those special moments, I learned to take an interest in what interested her. That is what she remembers.

And remember, bonding with your daughter never includes bravado. Treat her like the lady you want her to become as she grows. Make no assumptions. Be a humble, loving father.

REMEMBER TO LISTEN

The times that you will spend with your daughter are investments; they are exclusive opportunities for you both. These are times of sharing that will not present themselves under normal or everyday circumstances. Again, we'll dive deeper into it in chapter 3, but the uniqueness of your daughter and the distinctive events you will share together will undoubtedly allow for any number of discussions and decisions on a range of topics you may never have considered or prepared for.

These discussions will mature as she does. There will be conclusions and decisions she will eventually make in her mind, based upon the topics you discuss. She will move from discussion to consideration to conclusion, and her decision will be based upon your leading and direction as you commit the time to her.

When you're in the moment, resist the urge to talk too much. Listen. This might engender more communication or produce what may be (at first) uncomfortable silence. In the end, though, you should be listening more than you are talking. Take my word for it. You will learn a lot when you remember to listen. God gave us two ears to listen—and only one mouth to speak.

WHAT TO SAY WHEN YOU DO SPEAK

When you *do* talk, make your comments and compliments about her more about her core attributes and *not* only her looks. It can become too easy for us as men, as dads, and as untrained male role models to go there. Resist it.

Comments like "You are the most beautiful girl in the world" sound great to us dads. After all, we are delivering a wonderful comment (whether it's true or not) to our little girl. What could be wrong with that? Unfortunately, delivering messages like that will inevitably lead to a feeling and a need for her to live up to that. When puberty and other changes take their effect on her face, body, and emotions, she will need to recall deeper expressions from you that are not solely tied to beauty. Without this, she can quickly fall into self-loathing, low self-esteem, and introverted personality struggles. These issues can quickly lead to additionally destructive habits and activities like bulimia, anorexia, and body dysmorphic. These are extreme and specific situations that Claire did not struggle with. If your daughter is dealing with any of these extreme issues, get professional help. Don't accuse, correct, or attempt to be the doctor; just get her the help she needs.

A better remark (gauged according to her age, of course) could sound something like "You know, Claire, I just love how caring and accepting you are toward others. It is a sign of a very self-assured and secure young lady" or "Claire, you have so many wonderful attributes. You're smart, pretty, caring, and funny. What a great package! Everyone wants to be around people who care" or "You often remind me of your mom. She is really smart, she loves people, and she is so pretty." The issue is not the proverbial beauty comment or compliment. The key here is to unlock her understanding of how you place greater importance on her inner and expressed attributes. You love her character, her heart, and her passion for others—and finally, you also happen to think she is pretty.

I LOVE YOU

This may fall within the category of the obvious, but for the sake of clarity, you should, as a dad who cares about and loves his daughter, tell her you love her. It is not enough to simply love her; you have to express that love, show that love, and declare that love.

Some families take that precious statement for granted. In cases like that, the father may, in fact, love and care for his children, but he falls short in the verbal expression of it for any number of reasons. Maybe you were raised in a family in which your father simply expected the children in the home to "know" that he loved them, so there was no reason in his mind to express the statement. Worse yet, you might be one who had an abusive, elusive, or absent father, and therefore, you did not hear "I love you" at any time. In either case, you need to acknowledge the power of those words in the life of a child—your daughter.

Expressing "I love you" to your daughter is fundamental, it is foundational, and it will be at the core of what she knows about you, fatherhood, and what will someday become the litmus test in her relationships. Tell her you love her every day. Don't miss that, Dad. Tell her you love her every day.

For me, each day, when the kids would leave for school or, in most cases, when I left for work, I'd hug them, give them a kiss on the cheek, and tell them I loved them. Sometimes, on particularly hard days for them (or me), I would approach them individually later in the day and ask, "When's the last time I told you I loved you?"—to which they would reply something like "This morning" or, with playful sarcasm, "The last time you said it." When they reply, I would always say, "Well, that is too long. I love you"—and then would give them a big hug.

As you consider this, it may sound silly or over the top, but I assure you, it never went unnoticed or unappreciated. It is a hallmark of sorts for me—something they know is a "Dad thing" and another connection and symbol of my commitment to them. It is simple and engaging, but at the core, it is reassuring—for everyone.

The ease and simplicity of this single line of communication, which will echo in the heart and mind of your daughter, will be juxtaposed with the hard and painful realities that come from *failing* to communicate your love. If you are silent on the subject of love, there will be another echo in her heart and mind on the subject. Rather than a comforting, reassuring, and powerful message that resounds, she will encounter restless echoes of doubt, want, and insecurity. Dad, you strengthen her with your words, so put "I love you" at the top of the list of things you communicate to her.

MAKING SOMETHING SPECIAL JUST BETWEEN YOU TWO

It may be an unassuming and uncomplicated thing but will still create something that is always held and experienced between only the two of you. This is not a physical object you are creating. It is a feeling, a reminder, a touchstone in her mind and heart that helps her to recall and stand assured of your love that you have expressed since before she can remember.

Here are a few of mine that I have with Claire:

✓ Every night when Claire went to bed, lying alone in her room with the lights out, I would go into an adjoining room (which for years was my bathroom) and knock quietly on the wall to the rhythm of "shave and a haircut": *knock, knock, knock, knock, knock.* If she was still awake, she'd knock in reply *knock, knock,* to the rhythm of "two bits." Perhaps the most difficult one I did with her was when she spent her final evening at home before she left for college. It was and is a modest connection just before sleep that reminds her she is still being thought of.

✓ In my letters, texts, or cards to Claire, I have always ended it with "XOXOX" (hugs and kisses). This is so straightforward, so basic, and so appreciated. Now, even as an adult, I can simply text "XOXOX" to her, and she receives the full import of my heart to her. Reassurance on a day when perhaps the world has not been kind is always a good time to send hugs and kisses.

✓ Our anytime, day-or-night greeting is a "European kiss" (which admittedly is exercised around the world and not exclusive to Europe). It became our standard when she began to recognize kissing as a romantic gesture in her prepubescent stage. Right or wrong, there comes a time when your daughter's thoughts related to kissing on the lips will become an amorous event and gesture. When I recognized that, I decided to help her distinguish between the two by creating this new way for us to kiss. I think a distinct separation between platonic and passionate is healthy and wise when it comes to a kiss.

So, one night, while Janelle and I were sitting with her at bedtime, I said, "Claire, now that you are becoming a young lady, I think we should kiss each other like they do in Europe." I demonstrated how they embrace and kiss each other on each cheek—left and then right.

She said, "So, I can't kiss you on the lips anymore?"

I said, "No. You are going to want to kiss a boy on the lips someday, and this will be our forever way to kiss and hug each other."

To this she replied, "That makes sense. Cool."

To this day, when we see each other, we hug and exchange kisses on the cheeks. That gesture was employed throughout her "teenage" years—without embarrassment because it was "cool," as opposed to a lip kiss that would be seen as "affectionate" or "weird" in the eyes of her peers.

✓ Something else I did (admittedly with both of my kids) with great success was "a little piece of tickle." When Claire was around two years old, for no particular reason, I would approach her, kneel down, and dig into my pocket, carefully stating, "Claire I found something I think you will want…" or "Claire, have you ever seen this before?" or "Claire, did you see this thing I picked up in the backyard today?"

While she would answer, I would slowly bring my hand out of my pocket. With my other hand, I would pinch my thumb and index finger together to appear as if I had to pick up something very small, like a gold-dust flake, from the palm of my other hand. As I retrieved the nonexistent thing from my hand, I would hold up my pinched fingers, looking at it like a jeweler might as he inspects a fine stone in the light. Once I had observed it carefully, I would declare, as if it were a newly discovered treasure, "Claire, it's a piece of tickle!" and immediately begin to tickle her with it. She loved it! It was fun for both of us and another special thing between us.

As you may expect, she didn't fall for it after the second time, but she still loved it when I did it. In fact, for years, she would inspire me to do it to her, and later to Blake, saying things like "Daddy, I think there is something in your pocket. Do you know what it is?" It was fantastic. And even though she knew the drill, she would act as if she didn't: running in place, giggling, and screaming as I would slowly draw my hand from my pocket. As our tradition continued, I would retrieve it from different pockets to throw her off the trail, but (of course) it did not work. It actually made her laugh even more because she was convinced she had broken the code, and Daddy was unable to fool her. Those were sweet moments in time.

✓ I have another "something special" that I will share in chapter 7, but I'll round out our first chapter together with this: Pray with your daughter! Share in something that is bigger than both of you.

Without hesitation, I acknowledge the role of our faith in God and His standards in the successful raising of our children. I do not possess the skill to do it on my own without failures and compromise—which I still have, despite my best efforts.

Praying with Claire began as simple, childlike prayers. That's a great place to start. Later, as time, maturity, and issues in lives grew, our prayers developed into deeper, more meaningful communiqués of lament and appeal. These were all mile markers in her faith journey, my walk with the Lord, and our connection to our Savior—and each other. It is without question the single most important thing you can do with your daughter.

If you're not a Christian and don't understand the process, value, or connection to the Creator of the Universe, the Alpha and Omega, there is another book for you: the Bible. It contains the greatest story ever told of Jesus Christ and how he came to seek and save the lost. I too was once lost, walking on my own wide path, but I was found, forgiven, and given a new life in Jesus Christ. I pray the same for you.

"For God so loved the world that he gave his one and only Son, that whoever believes in him shall not perish but have eternal life. For God did not send his Son into the world to condemn the world, but to save the world through him" (John 3:16–17).

SPEAKING OF PRAYER

Some years ago, I underwent my second spinal surgery. This one was a complicated anterior (front) entry surgery that would include a multilevel fusion, with extenuating factors that, in the end, extended the procedure into—and then beyond—seven long hours.

While the surgery itself was a success, I developed a nearly fatal blood clot that extended from my ankle up to my torso. Limiting the details for brevity's sake, my left leg was swollen to an enormous state and was dark purple. I was rushed into surgery and additional procedures that later included venous screens, stents, and more. All of this occurred while I received massive amounts of blood thinners and other treatments to prevent the clot from entering my lungs, heart, or brain. There was one goal: save my life.

Unfortunately, those same life-saving measures had an unexpected effect: I began to bleed internally from the surgery site and throughout my midsection. Within hours, I was bleeding out internally and from my surgery site, and I was completely distended (looking pregnant) with my own blood. Then, with blood transfusions and plasma, I was in and out of consciousness, only able to bear the pain for a few moments following morphine injections. A few minutes later, I was back on the roller coaster again, writhing in pain. The pain was beyond immense and was far worse than any back pain I had previously experienced (which was a tremendous amount). At one point, the hospital called Janelle at home and suggested she come to the hospital immediately, stating, "This could be it!"

Copious amounts of morphine, two additional days in the ICU, many prayers, and God's providential hand brought me home after nine days. Janelle recalls those days as "horrific," saying that my skin tone—normally a pink Scottish-English tone—was ash gray, and I "looked like death."

Enough said. We later received a copy of my hospital chart and were shocked to see it was 312 pages long. There was a lot going on during that week and a half.

I came home as a shell of my former self, having lost over forty pounds in nine days. I was completely immobile and anemic, relying on Janelle to handle literally every bodily need and function of mine. Only drinking water, I didn't eat for ten days. I was unable to walk for twenty days, and I did not leave my zero-gravity reclining chair, bed, or house for forty. A nurse was at our home for weeks, drawing my blood at least twice a day for a month and then once a week for six months. Those days and the months that followed were pure hell. As a result of this misery, I was never completely normal again.

During my time in the hospital, I refused to allow Janelle to bring the kids to see me. Claire was seven years old, and Blake was four, so besides not wanting them to see the "scary" environment of the ICU or the hospital itself, I was fairly certain that I would not survive. I did not want them to see me at the end, wasting away in a hospital bed. That is not melodrama. I just wanted out, and I wanted to be home.

My mother-in-law, Linda, had been taking care of the kids. The night I came home, she took them into their shared bedroom as Janelle brought me into the house. With Janelle's help, a sturdy walker, and my zero-gravity recliner, I was set, literally unable to move from that spot for the next twenty-four hours.

The kids said hello for a second and were immediately hit with the reality that I had intended to hide from them while in the hospital. They both had terribly gloomy and worried looks on their faces as my wife and mother-in-law took them away again to prepare them for bedtime. It was obvious they were frightened and anxious about what was to come.

When Janelle returned, she covered me with a blanket to keep me warm as well as to hide my leg and the huge blood-stained gauze bandages on my stomach. Just then, sitting in their room waiting, the kids began chattering and begging to see me. She went into the bedroom and said, "Dad needs to rest, so you need to just say good night." She took hold of Blake's hand and walked out of their room with both of them. What happened next changed me—and my outlook on parenting and prayer—forever.

Reclining in the living room with an enormously swollen and throbbing left leg raised high above my heart on a wedge-shaped pillow, and all the while feeling like death itself, I turned my head to the right and watched the three of them proceed from their room. I do not exaggerate when I describe this: it was somewhat ethereal. The lights were off in the house apart from their room, so as they walked out, their silhouettes blocked the light, causing it to surround their bodies.

As they came closer, my eyes locked with Claire's. She had a determined look on her face—no longer scared, worried, or nervous. She walked toward me with purpose, with authority, and with compassion. It was, and remains, like nothing I have experienced since. A few feet away, Claire broke away from Janelle and Blake and came directly to me. I'm not sure she heard Janelle blurt out, "Claire! Be careful!" However, she was not going to hug me or jump on my lap. She was going to pray for me.

As she made her final step, standing securely at my low-reclined side, she stood over me with outstretched hands, placed them on my head, and began to pray with authority. No one led her. No one encouraged her. She simply wanted to bring her daddy to the throne of her Heavenly Father.

I don't remember a single word of her prayer. I don't remember how long it was. I wish I did. I *do* remember the rich, immediate, and satisfying sense of calm, soothing peace, and deep, abiding love that came over me then. That I will *never* forget. I expect that it will be one of the many feelings we experience when we go to heaven.

This is a deeply personal, profound, and emotionally charged memory that I cannot share without tears, thankfulness, and awe. I share it for the first time publicly with you by means of this book so that you may know the power and one of the purposes of prayer. Claire was only seven years old, yet she knew her Savior; she trusted in His power, and she called upon Him to be with her daddy. Nothing compares to that moment.

Pray with your daughter. Teach her what it is to pray.

Time. Your first gift to her.

Chapter 1 Recap and Checklist

- ☐ The challenge—your challenge—is to board the train, to learn from the challenges, and to be your daughter's dad. Don't just claim the title. Earn it.
- ☐ Career, travel, and time: these three areas demand your attention and resolve. Your career is secondary to your daughter. Business travel should be limited during the early years. Time is not on your side. Spending time with your daughter will be your first and most valuable gift.
- ☐ Teatime, reading, homework, and musicals (and more) are all opportunities to demonstrate your love for her, expressed in time— even if it is something you don't want to be doing.
- ☐ She'll need your confirmation. This is a time in her life and yours when you retell the story of her essential characteristics.
- ☐ Remember to listen. When you listen to her, you are learning, and you are indicating respect and care for her. When you do speak, make your comments and compliments more about her core attributes and *not* only her looks.
- ☐ Tell her you love her, and do it often. Don't ever assume she knows you love her. Tell her.
- ☐ Create something special just between you two. It may be an unassuming and uncomplicated thing, but still create something that is always held and experienced between only the two of you—reminding her of your love and connection.
- ☐ Prayer: embrace it. Live a life of prayer, and pray with your daughter. Teach her what it is to pray. This lasting gift will change you both, and it could change the world.

The Beginning: Hold Her Tight

If you're anything like me, you were amazed, excited, and full of joy to welcome your daughter into the world, hesitating each time to let her go from your arms, your protection, your love. That is exactly the way it was for Claire and me. We were inseparable. I truly could not wait until I came home from work to be with her at the end of each day. She was my light and my reason for being—my love, my precious gift, my daughter, Claire.

My parents, in-laws, and other family and friends used to give me a hard time about letting other people hold her in those first few months. I thought I did a reasonable job in allowing others to enjoy a few moments with Claire, but I discovered later that I was not as equitable with Claire's time as I had envisioned. In fact, during her first Christmas (about three weeks after her birth), she spent most of the time snuggled inside my Cabela's ranch coat that I wore at night. She loved the warm, flannel-lined jacket that formed a cocoon of sorts. I was happy to oblige. That first Christmas ended with fond farewells from the rest of our family with a statement that would resonate for weeks: "Merry Christmas! Next time, bring Claire!" Apparently, she wasn't seen much by everyone—oops!

Well, as good as it is to want to hold your daughter, that is not the type of "hold her tight" that I want to encourage with you. This is more of the emotional, supportive, and courageous type of hold, the sort of hold that lasts a lifetime in her heart and mind when she thinks of you, her dad.

Before we jump in, allow me to address a specific "housekeeping" issue. We need to remember that being the best dad starts with being a great husband and copartner in the good, bad, and ugly parts of parenting. Specifically, I want to encourage those of you who are awaiting your daughter's arrival or those in the infant-through-toddler stage to man up!

It kills me when I hear men—although mostly I hear moms complaining about their men—tell me that they can do so many things around the house, but they draw the line at diaper changes. Really? Are you kidding me? Grow a set of man hands, and get busy with the business of parenting. From the delivery room to her last diaper, I was there. In fact, I was pretty good at it. I could change a diaper with speed and precision. Whether it was on the changing table, across my legs, on the couch, or on my truck's tailgate—liquid or solid or somewhere in between—I was a "diaper-changing fool" and proud of it.

When it comes to feeding and cleaning up after your child, just get it done. For Janelle and me, it was quite the fandango. There can be no more messy, picky, or fussy eater than Claire was when she was an infant and toddler. Set your excuse list aside because Claire has your little girl beat. When the Cheerios and banana pieces are spread around on the high-chair tray, or the milk is leaking out of the sippy cup and running down your favorite easy chair or leather sofa, try to remember how important she is in comparison to those material things (and your frustration), and work through it.

Here's a funny parenting reality check. One time, when Claire was around two years old, our house developed an absolutely nasty, sour, throat-gagging smell. We couldn't figure out what the smell could be coming from. It wasn't a dead rat or something stuck in the walls, but we were equally repulsed by its consistent breaches into our nostrils. It was horrid. We lit candles, sprayed air freshener, and cleaned the carpet. Nothing worked.

We searched all over the kitchen, the living room, her bedroom, the bathroom, the diaper depository, and the attic space—literally everywhere. Well, almost everywhere. About a month later—ironically, just as the smell subsided—I was moving the couch and floor lamp around, and a horrific shape emerged from the back corner of the couch (which I later became convinced was jammed up into the underwrapping of the couch by my fearless and mischievous daughter).

It turned out to be a putrefied, petrified, and at one time, a near-living form of what began as her sippy cup of milk that she had opened to allow Cheerios, banana pieces, and something else to swim freely together in gastronomic harmony. I removed the putrid mystery and never bothered to put it in the dishwasher. It went straight to the trash can outside.

Share the duty, men. Am I saying that your daughter will remember you changing her, cleaning up her messes (along with her technicolor food explosions)? No, but I *do* know your wife will remember it. That is one of the steps required of a good dad.

PROACTIVE IS PROTECTIVE

Speaking of duty, let's talk about protecting your precious gift. Don't just *hope* she is protected; plan on it. Be proactive. When you are proactive, you are being protective in the right way. I know there isn't a single one of you who would stand idly by and watch an escaped convict kick in your front door, take your daughter from her room, and walk out of your home with her kicking and screaming. But some of our omissions and permissive mistakes can leave her open to a world of hurt and pain. I'll cover this topic succinctly, although it should be painfully obvious to you already. If it's not, read, consider, and implement a new strategy for her safety. Protect her. Think proactively.

BABYSITTERS

As a young man, I saw my older sister making a few extra bucks here and there by babysitting young children within our family's friend circle. It looked like fun and worth the time and money (and it did not require the sweat equity my lawn mowing did), so I asked my mom to suggest me to her friends as a babysitter.

Weeks went by, and to my surprise, no one asked my mom for sitting help from me. Meanwhile, my sister was in great demand, so I asked my mom why this was happening. She explained that most people prefer a female to babysit their children. I didn't understand that either, so I asked why. She refrained from details, but simply said, "That's the way it is. You should just plan on earning extra money in another way."

As a teenager, in adulthood, and certainly once I became a father to Claire, it was all very clear to me. No boy, teenager, or man would be babysitting my daughter. The risks we all consider are heightened with males—although not mutually exclusive—and not worth the gamble.

Social changes have loosened that feeling with many in this modern society, so to many, I was an overprotective dad who was "paranoid" and "suspicious." I'll wear that badge with pride—and polish it on Sundays—if it means I prevented an odd, or overtly evil, event of profound proportions from happening to my daughter. That is why we only allowed my parents, Janelle's parents, or my sister to babysit Claire.

SLEEPOVERS

Here is a tougher one and certainly one that is bound to test the value and depth of your friendships or family connections. No sleepovers.

Simply put, we did not allow Claire to sleep over at anyone's home when she was a little girl (with the exception of my parents, Janelle's parents, or my sister). Did I think that any of our friends, our family members, or Claire's friends or their family members were child molesters? Emphatically, no! But our resolve was clear. As parents, you cannot know what may happen in an environment outside of your control, even if people you know and trust are the hosts. We could not regulate what *other* people may come over to a house on that same night. We *could* control one thing: where she would sleep overnight as a little girl. And we did that.

We've all heard the same recollection from news and other accounts of a child molester who was caught, only to discover that his actions were not limited to only one victim but in fact a number of kids prior to capture. Additionally, we find that his evil intentions were first tested and perfected within his own family-and-friends network.

Dad, you will never have a child molester, at any age, announce his intentions. He will never introduce himself to you as a physical and emotional risk to your daughter. He will never put himself in jeopardy by openly admitting his demented behavior to you or to anyone else who can stop him. To the contrary, he will appear the same nice, normal, and perhaps trustworthy man as you are. You will likely never know or perceive anything to the contrary or something especially different about him until it is too late.

It comes down to this: Do you value the approval and acceptance from friends and family over the life and liberty of your daughter? Make the right choice, Dad. Protect her.

INTERNET, SOCIAL MEDIA, AND CELL PHONES

I am not a "techno-hip" dad. I don't know (or care) how computers or their applications operate, even though I use them every day. It doesn't interest or concern me in the least. I am the type of guy who just wants it to work. That's it. So, when it comes to the Internet, social media, cell phones, and other forms of technology input that our kids deal with on a daily basis, my position is straightforward and uncomplicated. It looks like this:

Internet use (for school or personal): My wife and I believe Internet use should be limited, controlled, and never private. Janelle and I have unlimited control, administrative access, and electronic safeguards on all of our devices.

Social media (all forms): We are the weird parents you may have heard about, because we believe in no social-media use. None. That's right. Nothing. If you insist to the contrary, limit it to a family page where family and friends can keep in touch. While I do not do it, I understand the value of a family page where distant friends and relatives can be kept in the loop of your family's significant events. Including photos and details have their own risks, so temper your desire to broadcast everything you have.

Notwithstanding society's current mood on the subject, social media is not necessary. It is rarely pure and certainly not as effective and sincere as other forms of communication or information sharing. Wow, do we look like weird people to Claire's friends and their parents (and maybe even you.)

Yes, I know we are out of step with society on this one, but I do not see the redeeming value of its use. On the contrary, I am (as you are too) aware of hundreds of cases of social-media abuse (most go unreported) against girls from inside and outside of their friend network. It will not end now or in the future, so steer her away from it.

I don't see social media improving itself or the lives of its subscribers either. After all, if those unnamed companies refuse to prevent ISIS and other terrorists from posting their evil rants and actions worldwide or don't avert live broadcasts of malicious and criminal behavior by teens against children, what makes anyone think they will lift a finger to stop kids from bullying or shaming or to filter predatory use of their system? One might conclude that they are only interested in one thing: money from their advertisers and sponsors. You may also determine that your daughter's emotional health is not high on their list, but it should be at the top of yours.

In the end, I told our kids that they are free to participate in any form of social media they desire once they leave our home and are on their own. Until then, they can communicate face-to-face or through e-mail, text, or a revolutionary device called a *phone*.

Cell phones: Janelle and I believe that age fourteen is a good age for cell phones. This may differ for you and your social, sports, travel, or family communication needs, but that is the age that we permitted it. Additionally, Claire and Blake both understood the parameters of use and of our administrative, nonprivate, and universal control of their device and their communication.

Our children grew up in Orange County, California (in the middle of "Yuppie World USA," in my estimation). We were different from many of our contemporaries in a number of ways. We sacrificed to provide for a private-school education and environment. Because of that type of education and the communities it served, our kids were around other families who ranged from upper middle class to well-to-do to legitimately rich.

While I do not attribute the following phenomenon to families of above-average income alone, it did seem especially prevalent—and, in our view, problematic—in her peer group and others in this area.

Claire's friends began receiving cell phones from their parents in the second grade. I am not talking about letting your child play video games on your phone to keep them busy or giving them your "old" phone to call Grandma and Grandpa from time to time. No. She had friends who were receiving next-generation, brand-new cell phones and were taking them to school with them. It was crazy to us.

Let's face it, most kids who have cell phones prior to fourteen are just going to download and play video games, take part in social media or messaging, surf the web, or do other nonessential activities that can be done somewhere else. They don't need them, so take control of that aspect of their growth, and decide what is right for them. Don't let society make that decision.

SPEAK SOFTLY

There will be any number of times in your daughter's young life when she will test your nerves, strain your patience, and challenge your resolve. In those moments, choose to speak softly. The time will come when you must put your foot down and raise your voice to address an unruly or disrespectful moment in her preteen or teen years. For your part, make sure you can count the explosive times (though justified in your mind) on one hand.

Avoid cutting remarks or unkind words at all costs. The words we use toward our daughters will last a lifetime. You are either speaking peace and strength into her life or you are cutting away at the roots of her core and very being. Words matter, Dad.

Your daughter is a gift. She is a tender heart and a soul worth protecting—especially from your anger. Speak softly when you know you should.

READ *FOR* HER, NOT JUST *TO* HER

Reading *for* her means that you invest additional time and effort along the way to read books, articles, and other related materials that educate and empower you to be a better dad. I happen to be an avid reader and have read a few hundred books as an adult, the subject matter ranging from professional to historical, family to children, as well as a few specifically on daughters. If you're not a reader, make the exception here. As men, we don't know it all. We must admit that and get on with it.

It doesn't take much effort to find any number of "great books for Dad" nowadays. That said, my favorite source for reference is Amazon (along with a few hundred million other happy customers), so unlike in years past when you had to search the bookstore shelves wondering which book was best for your specific need, now we all benefit from the reviews (and fast shipping).

The question I am asked all the time is, "What single book would you recommend I read to get a better handle on my daughter and my role?" (Funny, because I should suggest this book now that it is in print.) My answer will remain the same as it has been for years: *Strong Fathers, Strong Daughters* by Meg Meeker, MD. There are so many others; some I've read or surveyed, and others I haven't, but if you only read one book (other than this one), it must be Dr. Meeker's. I have given that book to more people than any other book. Literally, if you have a girl, and you and I are friends, count on a copy coming in the mail or being handed to you by me. It is a jewel, an encouragement, and a must read.

LETTERS OF LOVE, ENCOURAGEMENT, HOPES, AND DREAMS

It goes without saying that if you want to earn the title of "Dad," you should certainly begin by displaying love, providing consistent encouragement, celebrating her hopes and aspirations, and making a conscious effort to inspire her and free her to dream. There are so many ways to do this, and most of them will be discovered, learned, and refined along the way. But one long-term strategy I have used to this day is writing letters to Claire. This comes in two forms. First are the notes, cards, e-mails, and letters I send to her from time to time to connect with her or to address specific events or milestones in her life.

The second, and what I will focus on here, are the "letters of love" that I have been writing—and that remain unopened—since before Claire was born.

When Janelle was pregnant with Claire, I went through my own set of hormonal changes. I cried in a theater while watching *Driving Miss Daisy* because it reminded me of my grandmother when she went into a nursing home. I would watch people scold their child in public for perfectly good reasons and with proper application of correction, but I'd find my heart breaking for the child, trying to see his or her side of the story and the misbehavior. And no matter what level of punishment was meted out, I felt like it was too severe, as if perhaps the parent was taking the gift of that precious child for granted. (Don't worry; I came to my senses when Claire came. She was a handful, and we meted out plenty of in-home and public applications of correction.) During the ebb-and-flow emotions in the pregnancy months, I went through a period where I felt woefully unprepared—to the point of feeling inept— for Claire's arrival and my roles and responsibilities as her father. These feelings developed into a need to express my love, care, and dreams for Claire *to Claire*. To tell her how much I loved her already; to convey my hopes, aspirations, and dreams for her life; to voice what was erupting inside my heart for her; to let her know that I was already holding her in my arms, wiping her tears, and giving her my heart even before she arrived. But how?

While on a business trip to Pennsylvania, I resolved to actually write some of my thoughts and feelings down—whatever came to mind, stream-of-consciousness sort of writing—and see where it went. So I sat down at the table, pulled out the hotel's stationery, and got to work. What seemed like just a few minutes later was actually two hours. It took longer than expected, but it felt great. The next morning, I addressed, sealed, and mailed the letter to a yet unborn "Miss Claire Elizabeth Arnold."

When I returned home, Janelle, holding the letter, smiled and asked, "What's this?"

I explained, saying, "We'll just put it in the safe so she can read it someday." And so we did.

As it turns out, the desire to share so many things with Claire even once she arrived was so great that I began to look forward to mailing her a letter from time to time when I had to travel for work or volunteer at events and meetings. Over the years, the letters came from a number of states and foreign countries. They comprised events of the day: thoughts I had of her; things she was doing at her particular stage of growth; and my hopes and dreams for her as an infant, a toddler, a young lady, a teenager, and into her adult years as a college student and beyond.

Whenever possible, I would retrieve the recent family photo or her school picture that I carried in my wallet and insert it into the envelope as an additional time-capsule reference.

The letters became a touchstone of sorts for me and hopefully someday will be the same for her. They confirmed my attendance to and recollection of her life's journey up to that date and were a foolproof way to record my love, my heart, and my prayers for her.

It also occurred to me (as one who has a number of significant health issues) that if I would pass away before one of those significant life stages (which I now simply recall because that did *not* happen), she would have a tangible set of documents—evidence, if you will—of "Dad and his love for me."

Even if someday I were to receive a diagnosis of Alzheimer's disease (like others in my family), be crippled with a stroke that limits my communication, or die at whatever age, I want Claire to know exactly how I felt about her every step of the way, how much I loved her, and how my words would be an everlasting proof and reassurance of my love and acknowledgment of the gift that God had given me.

Realizing the depth of this thing called parenthood—and specifically becoming your daughter's daddy—may move you to do something similar. Maybe not. Perhaps for you it is something entirely different and more creative. Whatever it is, just do it.

Sitting in my safe today, a bound stack of letters addressed to Claire is waiting to be opened. When? I have not decided, but I am leaning toward a post-college-graduation gift, wanting it to be something other than a textbook for her to read. That will be a special day.

Chapter 2 Recap and Checklist

☐ Share the duty, men. Your care of her starts with getting dirty. Get in there, and be Dad.

☐ Protect her. Think proactively. Think ahead of the problem, and keep her safe.

☐ Babysitters. Be more than selective; be ruthless.

☐ Sleepovers. Unless it is the trusted grandparents, skip it.

☐ Internet. Limited, controlled, and never private.

☐ Social media. If you insist, then it should only be a family account. No individual accounts.

☐ Cell phones. Age fourteen at the earliest.

☐ Speak softly. No cutting remarks. Your daughter is a gift. She is a tender heart and soul worth protecting—especially from your anger. Speak softly when you know you should.

☐ Read *for* her and not just *to* her. Invest additional time and effort along the way to read books, articles, and other related materials that educate and empower you to be a better dad.

☐ Letters of love, encouragement, hopes, and dreams are an opportunity for you to record your thoughts, prayers, and awe of her at the specific moments of time that you will both fail to remember at some point in your lives. Document those times, those thoughts, and all of your love, whether in a letter or in some other form of time capsule. Do it, and watch how special it is—both when you write them and when she reads them.

3

The Early Years: Displaying Love, Respect, and Chivalry

When Claire was young, she was a handful. Scratch that—she was several large, strong, forceful handfuls that kept Janelle and me very busy, worried, and tired. These types of children—not to mention girls—can be hard for parents to figure out. The game plan for the independent, inquisitive, and fearless little girl was not in the daddy playbook I had tucked away in my head. For better or worse, Janelle and I had to figure out much of it on our own. However, one thing never wavered: our love.

For us, the playbook of parenting has a few other tabs you need to reference along the way. Tied to the love that you should demonstrate and validate, making the effort to show respect and be chivalrous is another important fatherly characteristic. Don't tune out now; there is a method to this process.

From about eighteen months until she was around nine years of age, if Claire was presented with a physical obstacle of any imposing shape or size (e.g., a boulder alongside a hiking trail or a tree that had a low limb she could reach, sometimes with the help of her six-foot-four dad, or jump around in the open bed of my truck), Claire was all over it. She was intrepid, resolute, and quite audacious. I have no idea where all of that came from, but Janelle and my parents are pretty sure *they* know.

In fact, from about nine months on, Claire preferred to be carried by me when we were out (we think it was because the view was better up high). She could be thrown up and down on a whim, tickled without warning, or be lifted onto my shoulders for a commanding observation of her surroundings as she got older. But at some point, around eighteen months or so, she began to think beyond the standard infant-and-toddler leg kicks and twitches while she was carried on our hips, graduating to a full thrust or—as I used to warn Janelle when I would observe it coming— "preparation for launch!"

Claire would see something she wanted to investigate or play with, and with surety of purpose and spirit, she would fix her little feet to each side of the hip of whoever was carrying her, something like a "squatting" or "deep knee bend," and, with great speed and strength, spring out of our arms as she leaped toward the object of her desire— just like a monkey jumping from limb to limb in a tree. Because this very troubling habit began when she did not possess the strength, skill, or timing required to accomplish the "launch," we trained ourselves to keep a weary hold on her thigh whenever she was being carried—until one very scary day.

It was a Sunday morning. Claire was on my hip, and we were mere feet away from entering our church's lobby doors when she noticed something in the flower gardens along the walkway. Before I could react with a tight grip, she literally sprang into action. She vaulted off my hips in a sideways "I can fly!" sort of launch, leaving her airborne. She had successfully escaped my secure hold and was in flight, heading face first toward the concrete planter.

Like a scene from *The Matrix*, the events seemed to unfold in slow motion. At the same time, with catlike (or what I describe as "Claire-like") reflexes, I reached out with my right hand and caught her left thigh while she was in her midtrajectory dive, snatching her back to me like a chameleon's tongue. She was safe. Janelle and I were in shock.

Raising your daughter is a lot like that. You can be doing all the right things and cruising along, but then a new and unexpected event or obstacle comes your way, and you must deal with it in real time, which is always faster than we would prefer. But you *can* prepare the foundation of your relationship, all the while offsetting some of life's surprises. So let's talk about the foundation that she will rest secure in until that unexpected day comes.

DISPLAYING LOVE

You may or may not have been raised in a loving and secure home. Regardless, the relationship that you witnessed between your father and your sister may *not* be what you desire for you and your daughter. You may simply have no reference or experience at displaying love and don't know inherently what it takes to get it done right. Whatever position you find yourself in, the foundations of your deep and abiding relationship will always begin with love. Love your daughter enough to display it.

I've been around men who, for any number of personal reasons, fail at every turn to display, convey, or provide a loving foundation to their children. It is so sad, painful, and detrimental to the emotional health and well-being of their kids, but it is especially hard on their girls. Girls require a few things—not to the exclusion of boys, of course—that *only* dad can deliver. I submit to you that on the list of foundational needs, there is love, respect, and chivalry.

When a dad displays love toward his daughter, she inherently becomes more secure in her own space. She knows that her protector, likely the only hero in her life at this juncture, is in love with her as a person, as his daughter, and as his very special gift that has been entrusted to him by God. She needs your love, men. It is a foundation you need to build with purpose.

Whatever foundation of love that you feel you missed out on or did not get enough of or didn't receive the right kind of, give *that* to her—and more. Your daughter deserves to be the beneficiary of all that you can give her—and all that you may *not* have received, if that is the case. Double down on love; it will come back to you. Even if it never came back to you, give her all the love you can.

RESPECT

Respecting your daughter is as important as expecting it from her. No, I don't mean a self-deprecating worship of your daughter's mere presence before you. I am not referring to the soft, effeminate, or disciplinary-reticent dad who tiptoes around his daughter. I am not talking about any of the modern psychology rants about giving your children equal say in matters that most of us would agree are adult decisions. No, I simply refer you to the basic definition of *respect*.

Respect—such as esteem, regard, and honor—is important. When you respect your daughter, her place in the family structure, and her value to society at large, you allow her to develop a normal, emotionally secure, and happy character, who in turn looks after others and is not self-absorbed or lacking a personal compass. In addition, when you show respect to your daughter, she will accept it and *not* seek it from the wrong places or people. I know far too many girls who, not having the respect of their fathers expressed to them, embark on heartbreaking journeys that never result in contentment. Most end in pain and remorse.

Without Dad's respect, some girls in more extreme cases grow up to be promiscuous, while others take on the male role in their own relationships to "right a wrong" and be in control, and still some, as adults, literally kill themselves to prove their worth in the career world. They leave their own children, husband, and core responsibilities (for hours or for a lifetime) for the value, position, and promotion the boardroom provides. That scenario is all too prevalent nowadays.

I have watched it change, challenge, and destroy marriages and families of people I love and care for deeply. For what? Money, position, things? No. At the core, those same women just want respect, and I would submit it should come from their fathers first. Men, give her the foundational respect she deserves now so she doesn't spend her adult years looking for it in other ways.

Finally, men, show your wife respect. Respecting your wife is key to building a healthy foundation. If you demonstrate respect toward your wife—even your ex-wife, if that is the case—you signal to your daughter what is proper and expected of *her* future husband. If you show respect to your wife and daughter, the likely outcome is that she will choose a man who respects her. In the case of an ex, separation, or disillusionment, it may require that you "fake it." Do it then. Your daughter is watching.

CHIVALRY

Chivalry is *not* dead! If it died or is on life support in your home, revive it immediately!

Chivalry as a word is not used much anymore, but understanding its place in her life and your relationship is important. *Chivalrous* could share its purpose with words we use more regularly, like *courageous, brave, gallant, loyal, courteous, polite, attentive,* and *considerate.* Persons of valor, heroism, fearlessness, and spirit are ones who stand out in our fallen world. These are the descriptors of the man you want her to become attracted to, marry, and someday have her own children with.

Let me assure you of something, men: if you do *not* project these qualities, she is less likely to seek these same attributes in her husband. Be the example of what you want your son-in-law to be.

So how does chivalry look from your daughter's perspective? Well, it is clearly related to her age and what you can display for her observation and absorption. When she was a little girl, I would act out fun vignettes of chivalry that she could be amused by so that as her maturity developed, the basics of the concept were already there, and I could build on it in a matter-of-fact way. Let me share an example.

When it would rain, or if there were sprinkler puddles in our way as we walked, I would sometimes say, "My lady, I don't want your shoes to get wet, so I must carry you away!" And with that, I'd whisk her off her feet and soar her over the puddle. It was always good for some giggles, and it served two purposes: it gave her a picture of chivalry and her dad's care as well as keeping her from doing what she loved to do anyway—stomping in puddles!

As Claire grew older, I would take her hand to cross the street (even though she was "big enough") or to navigate a congested space of people in the mall. The opportunity to be chivalrous will come to you, but that doesn't mean you can't plan a demonstration. Sprinklers, puddles, or minefields of leaves on the lawn—you choose, but demonstrate chivalry to your daughter.

Use the simple moments in her life to show her you're her hero and why. Be fearless, and kill a few spiders for her. Lift up her mattress like a superhero when she asserts "something bad" is hiding underneath it. Demonstrate how men should treat ladies by being courteous, polite, and attentive when she has something to share with you (even when it sounds like the mind-numbing babble that kid talk sometimes is). Be patient. When you're not patient, you're not listening or learning.

Exhibit your loyalty in the little things. When you commit time to her—whether dressing dolls together, playing outside, or reading to her—don't let another adult or circumstance come into that, especially when it is something you'd *rather* do. Canceling a play date with her because your buddies invited you to play eighteen holes at your favorite green is totally unacceptable. When the phone rings, including your cell phone, do not accept the call. Show her that your time with her is special. It is an appointment you keep, and it is uninterrupted.

Just as with love and respect, you must also be chivalrous with your wife. Some of you may need to rekindle, recharge, or revamp the chivalrous side of yourself, but you need to do it. You may not be able to "whisk her" over a puddle anymore, but you can still kill a few spiders and slay a few "clean the toilet" dragons for her along the way. Your daughter is watching.

Fact: Ask Janelle or my children who cleans the toilet. Answer: Shad.

Chapter 3 Recap and Checklist

☐ Displaying love is foundational. Your daughter deserves all of your love. If you did not receive love, or not enough of it, as a child, she is the present reality that allows you to express all of that and more to her. Let her be the beneficiary of all that you have and all you wanted as a child.

☐ Respecting your daughter is as important as expecting respect from her. Don't fail in this effort, Dad. Girls need to be respected by their fathers so they don't grow up looking for it in other men. Showing your wife respect should be the standard by which she gauges relationships.

☐ Chivalry is not dead. Show her what a hero, a courageous man, and a real father look like by being chivalrous. Kill a few spiders, carry her over a puddle or two, and remember to demonstrate chivalry with your wife along the way.

4

Building the Young Lady

I t's time to build your little girl into a young lady. But how? Pardon the construction metaphor, but most guys like construction, so I'll apply it to your daughter in this case to flesh out the concept. If your daughter was a building, there would be a conceptual design phase, architectural and structural design specifications, and various engineering tasks and modeling, and after some permits and payments to the design and construction teams, the core and shell of the building would commence.

With or without prior building (parenting) experience, you wouldn't dare grab some heavy equipment, graders, pylon drivers, or a bunch of steel and concrete and start work on the building you've always wanted. Of course not. No. You would hire an architect, develop the concept, initiate the design-and-specification stage, contract with engineers, hire a general contractor, and in time, bring on any number of contractors to bid on and eventually construct your building to code and to your satisfaction. Is parenting any different in your mind? It shouldn't be. It is a process—specific steps toward the goal of building your little girl into a young lady.

One key similarity to the building process are the limitations set forth. Whether it is your vision, your budget, or your property boundaries, you have limitations to deal with. The architect sets a limit on the number of floors and the square footage of the building based on any number of other factors that you may not have considered. The electrical, structural, plumbing, and HVAC engineers fix their own set of limits on the building process. The general contractor places limits on the way the construction is undertaken, in order to adhere to code and safety guidelines. In your case, you are the designer, engineer, contractor, building owner, and manager. You must set limits—limits on external influences, commitments to extraneous activities, unsavory behavior, and the like.

When it comes to discipline, you and your wife need to have a "meeting of the minds" and come to a mutual agreement on the proper level and application of discipline during each life stage or age your daughter is in. Some couples are apprehensive about this process because they were likely both raised "differently"—a factor that always brings tension in the parenting process. However, if you do not set limits, your daughter will. You do not want her to set her own limits. It's not correct, healthy, or reasonable for her to assume that role. Just as in our construction metaphor, you need to set the limits so that she knows exactly what is expected, what is permissible, and what is absolutely unacceptable.

There was a short period of time when Claire was young that Janelle and I were absolutely at our limits with Claire's testing, provocation, and disobedience. It required a "breaking of her spirit." No, I don't mean like tying up a wild mustang until it collapses. Rather, we had to come together as parents to set limits that she would have to stay within, or we would have lost her down a rabbit hole of disobedience and disappointment. We purposed in our hearts what the limits were and where we would set them—and we stayed committed. Claire adapted, changed because of the limits imposed, and matured into a spectacular young lady in the process.

We'll skip over the simple and mundane "limits" you will need to address as a parent, such as bedtime, playtime, healthy eating, and so on. What I will say is this: lead in the bigger things. Work on the foundation of your "building" and make it strong, secure, and assured. When you identify the details that limit her from getting off track, you are grading; forming; pouring; and ultimately setting the strong, sure, solid foundation for life-long success.

RESPECT AT ALL TIMES

In the last chapter, we discussed respect. Respect, in your daughter's case, is different from yours, of course, but it's required all the same. We have an entire generation of people in America—and I am sure around the world— who are completely void of respect for others. Many are simply animals who were released from their cages and expected to join the society they failed to connect to and with for the first eighteen years of their lives. It is a shining example of the failures of the parents, the coddling of the school system, and a general disregard and misdirection by society at large. If your daughter is not taught, shown how, and expected to be respectful, when and how will she ever be?

If your daughter does not have respect for herself, she will be incapable of showing respect for others. Engender respect by respecting your wife and daughter. Then you can and should expect (dare I say demand) the same *from* your daughter. This is as simple as "monkey see, monkey do." When your daughter is living within a familial bond of love and respect, it is nearly impossible to end up with a rude, self-absorbed, and disrespectful girl.

When Claire and Blake were young, we simply did not allow them to display any level of disrespect to others, especially adults. Disrespect was absolutely an ironclad, guaranteed ticket aboard the pain train (we are talking about a spanking or other appropriate correction). Children who even as toddlers are allowed to disrespect others, particularly adults, become quite selfish, narcissistic, and apathetic. If you allow her to ignore, not give full attention to, or even make rude or uncharitable comments toward others, you are allowing her to build her own foundation of indifference.

I invested nearly twenty-five years of my adult life volunteering within an international youth program, serving in various local, district, and national-level positions. Since the program served children aged from five to nineteen, over those years of service, I met, interacted, and worked with (sometimes on a weekly basis) kids from all walks of life, socioeconomic statuses, and calibers of parents. In some cases, I watched a few grow from kindergarten through college, get married, and have children of their own.

I've had the honor of working with some of our nation's finest youth and the occasion to see some of their counterparts. I can say without reservation that the vast majority of "problem" kids I came across in my experience, there and elsewhere, were at their core devoid of respect, while the remainder were simply disrespectful. What they were caught doing or what came of their mischief was secondary; they were nearly all disrespectful people. At the risk of sounding like a crotchety old school principal from a puritan era gone by, I think respect is key. If your daughter does not show it, she certainly will not receive it, creating a larger issue for both of you as she moves into her teenage years. I'll touch on that again in chapter 8 when we cover dating.

Please pardon the delivery of these brief quotes. They are not meant to inform you of how awesome my children were or are, but throughout our parenting years, people and other parents would say things like, "Wow, your kids are so mature and respectful," or "Your kids are so well behaved," or "I wish I could get my kid to be calm and respectful around adults like your kids are," and most commonly, "What's your secret? They are so different from other kids their age. They are just so respectful."

So here is the secret. Do not permit anything but respect at all times and in all situations. Do not confuse that with application of excessive discipline or directed anger. Do not confuse it with blind obedience without thought, because that is called a robot, and we definitely didn't raise robots (and I hope you don't either). Rather, make it a matter-of-fact issue with her. Disrespect will *not* be tolerated at any level, at any time. She will respond to that faster than you might imagine, and before you know it, people will share the same awe-filled observation with you about your children.

Let me mention a side note. Someone may read this and wonder if my children ever questioned our decisions or authority, or if they were mind-numbed and obedient minions at all times. No. They were not obedient minions, but the answer is yes, both of my kids *did* question our decisions and authority—and were allowed to.

Now you are really confused, right? It's actually quite simple. Our kids were allowed to call a family meeting or call a parent meeting anytime to air grievances, protest what they thought was unfair about something, or even just ask something of Janelle and me—conversations that, outside of the confines of the parent meeting, would have been received as disrespectful, disobedient, or otherwise. If our kids had something to say that was contrary to what we had said, it was allowed within the guidelines of our family unit. It was no different from a student being permitted to speak aloud in class once called upon or you driving through an intersection when the light is green.

There is wisdom in setting boundaries for foundational ingredients like respect. Those who would read this far and consider that we must have been overly firm, mean, or overtly dictatorial with our children to elicit the type of result I described would be wrong—dead wrong. And for Claire's part, she defined, lectured, and toured the country demonstrating the "terrible twos." She broke our heart and parental spirit on a number of occasions, but we were determined to see her through this phase and not allow it to be a lifelong pursuit. We wanted more for her, and we loved her enough to hold fast to what was right. She was a Tasmanian devil socially for some time and ruined a number of events and outings for Janelle and me, but we committed to fixed, resolute, loving correction and guidance, promising each other we would not give up! Further, the parents whom you see allowing their children to break every rule or conversation between adults are the same ones who will grow up believing *they* are the center of everything. That may be the beginning of the so-called "snowflake" generation. We can do better, men. Start with your daughter.

THANK YOU, BEING THE STANDARD

Men, there is another very specific and essential portion of your daughter's foundation that you're building in her early years. You must teach her to be thankful. You must teach her to express that thanks. Make it a standard—not the *adjective* definition that includes "normal" or "ordinary," but the *noun*. Making it a standard for her means that "thanks" is the benchmark, the model, the guideline, the requirement, and the specification. Make it a foundational truth, Dad.

Sure, we all tell our kids, "What do you say? Say, 'thank you,'" when they are presented with a gift by someone, because kids can have the tendency to stare at or play with the gift before their heart and brain align to tell them that it was a gift, meaning they should be thankful. I am talking about a diverse application of "thanks"—being thankful all the time and in most situations.

Teach her that "thank you" is her standard for life. When people try but fall short, she needs to respond gratefully, saying, "Thank you for trying." When she drops her pencil in class, and a classmate picks it up and hands it to her, she should tell them, "Thank you." When the teacher spends a few additional moments explaining the correct path of a complex equation, "Thank you for taking extra time for me" is the correct response. When her coach encourages her to practice more because it will pay off in time, encourage her to say, "Thanks for the encouragement, Coach! I needed that." When her emotions, experiences, and unrealistic expectations collide in a horrible wreck at the blind intersection of Teenage Lane and Real-Life Road, saying, "Thanks for being there and listening, Dad! I love you!" would go a long way. You'll recognize it as a standard then, and so will she.

GIVE HER A PAYCHECK, NOT AN ALLOWANCE

Janelle and I continued on with a program that my parents began with my sister and me decades earlier: a paycheck, not an allowance. When it comes to making a few extra bucks when they are young or simply doing their chores, a paycheck is always a better program and foundation for your kids. The difference is that an allowance is a grant, a stipend, or a preestablished budget, while a paycheck is remuneration, a payment, and an earned salary or income.

Here's how it works. For the standard work of being part of the family, like keeping her room cleaned up, making her bed, and putting away toys, she gets a standard paycheck. As she gets older and takes on more responsibility (in Claire's case, she fed and cared for more than thirty lay-ing hens—cleaning their coop, washing the eggs, and more—from about fifth grade until she left for college), she gets paid more. The recipient of a paycheck also has the opportunity to earn bonuses. So if I were, for example, painting a room, and Claire wanted to earn some extra money (a bonus, over and above her standard responsibilities), I might assign her the taping and clean-up job and pay her accordingly.

Here is where the foundational lessons are learned. If their work is in-complete, poorly done, or they have to be told repeatedly to do it, they can be paid less, not paid at all, or even docked pay—just like in the *real* world. (Hint: Once they figure that out in real time, it will not happen again.) Both of our children have been docked for not doing their standard jobs or for neglecting an important facet of their job, such as filling the water bowls for the dogs in the middle of summer. It only happens once for them to get with the program, because either way, they know it must be done, so they might as well get paid for it.

Another basic, obvious, and enduring part of the paycheck program is that they don't grow up with a snowflake idea that "I deserve it," "That should be provided to me for free," and other entitlement attitudes. They learn that real work has a benefit to it: cash and self-respect.

HER "FIRST DATE"

First date? "What does that have to do with building foundations and my little girl's emotional growth?" you may ask. I understand your confusion, but stick with me here.

Let's say your daughter goes on her first date at age thirty—okay, twenty-five. Seriously, maybe it is as early as eighteen. In any case, when that day comes, you will be prepared, and more importantly, so will she. So, all kidding aside, her "first date" is with you. Be ready.

When Claire was two, it was common for me to come home from work and give Janelle a break. If you already have children—and especially if they are in the "terrible twos"—you know just what I'm talking about.

Janelle needed a break as much as Claire needed a change of scenery, and in the end, they both appreciated the brief time away.

What began as an hour or two of daddy-daughter time in the afternoon once in a while developed into an opportunity to enjoy one-on-one time, discover new things together, and learn more about each other. I threw away the rules during the moments Claire and I shared together. The only hard-and-fast rule was this: no rules. We could go to the park and play and end up with grass-stained clothes, and it was okay. We could get ice cream just before dinner, and it was okay. We could talk about silly stuff and make too much noise, and it was okay. Generally speaking, we could do what we wanted to; it was our time.

One of our favorite spots to go was a Baskin-Robbins ice-cream shop in the City of Orange. I grew up close to it, about a mile away, and I recall the relatively few instances my sister and I succeeded in convincing one of our parents to take us there for a single scoop. You remember, don't you? The myriad flavors, the cool temperature of the store, and the smell of crème heaven. Think about it: ice cream has a smell. As in a bakery or a donut shop, you can smell the product they are selling. Kids remember that sort of thing. Decades later, so do *adults*.

This particular Baskin-Robbins had outside seating that had been constructed using their trademark pink—Claire's favorite color at the time. We preferred sitting together outside unless it was too hot, because we liked to watch the cars and people go by and could talk without disturbing anyone.

When we arrived, Claire would always pull me into the store, begging me to hurry in so she could survey the entire ice-cream case. Inevitably, though, she would focus in on her favorite: strawberry. I would order a small cup (which she called a "baby cup") of strawberry ice cream with a few added sprinkles (of course) and two Baskin-Robbins pink spoons. In fact, in those early years, we would use the sample spoons because it made the little scoop of ice cream in the "baby cup" look bigger (one of my "dad tricks"), stretching it out further.

Our delicate conversations slowly melt away in my mind as I consider the decades past, and while I can't recall much of what was discussed beyond the usual line of dollies, bugs, and pretty dresses, I *do* remember it was profound for her. I *do* recollect that the times were so very sweet to me—so much sweeter than the ice cream or sprinkles, to be sure. I will admit to you that I reminisce about those times and hold them tight to my heart like the hugs we shared together back then. Some moments and memories of those times evoke profound emotions for me. When I concentrate on the memory of her hair; her little hands; and her hugs, kisses, and giggles, it can break me. It's good to be broken like that from time to time.

You see, it was more than just ice cream. It was more than just time. It was ice cream with Daddy and time well spent. It was silly talk and giggles with her hero, her dad. It was a time to step away from both of our schedules and commit to special time together. It was a window into the future—whether we knew it or not. It was another touchstone in her life that would bring her heart to silent confirmation of the love, respect, and future that we dreamed for her then. What began simply as an opportunity to give Janelle a break became a deep and satisfying occasion that made an astonishing impact on my relationship with Claire.

At one point, I determined that I would calendar our time together, so that once a month, it would be just Claire and me. It would again be a time where we could talk, listen, share, giggle, and some years later, cry together. These times would be rock-solid, ironclad, immovable dates and times on the calendar that she knew were just for her. This became even more important as she grew older, when Blake, school, and other things pulled at her time and mine.

With very few exceptions, those dates remained on the calendar and were adhered to. In the few instances where our scheduled "date" was in jeopardy, I did not relocate our date without Claire's input. If I had a business trip or event that got in the way, I gave Claire the right—the absolute right—to relocate our date on a day that worked for her. Remember to do the same, Dad.

Setting the time aside was the first step. Second would be the purpose. I resolved to make these times foundational—fun, of course—but lasting in their reason. We referred to them as "daddy-daughter dates," and later just "daddy dates," and finally, "our dates," because throughout the years (in addition to our relational growth together), it was an opportunity to show Claire how boys, and later a man, should interact with her. Opening doors for her, guiding her through dense crowds, or walking into stores that *she* liked, and not because it was what I preferred, were all part of the process.

Our dates, whether over dinner or walking the mall, would be characterized and remembered as enjoyable, yet teaching-filled moments about foundational truths. Claire's faith, her purpose, and how others fit into the life that God had given her to live were all on the table. There were never any secrets or off-limits discussions; she was free to ask, share, and even disagree with me. As the years went by, we would speak of topics and problems (that some dads might run from) as casually as we would the weather because the foundations of love, respect, trust, and more had already been laid years before.

This was a seminal discovery, born of a simple plan to spend quality moments of time with my daughter. Time, purpose, and freedom are what every teenager wants and what most cannot handle on their own without disappointment. Claire would experience those things in the safety of a father's embrace and overwatching counsel, learning to dialogue about good and bad, things that made her happy, and things that made her sad. This thing we called our "date" was to be a common thread between us that no one person or circumstance could cut. We were bonding and growing together, and it has galvanized our relationship beyond any measure.

When Claire left for college, we went on our last date for a while. It was hard for both of us. Later, on a visit home, she texted me with her train details and asked, "Are we going to go on a date while I am home?" Validation.

My strongest encouragement comes to you now, men. Take your daughter on a "daddy-daughter date." Whatever her age, put it on the calendar, and keep it. Show her how a man treats his lady, and be age-specific in your conversation and foundational work. Open her door, be her prince, display loyalty and honesty, be attentive, be chivalrous, and love her. Be Dad!

ROAD TRIPS TOO

Girls love fun and adventure too. As men, I think too many of us are prone to taking our boys out or going out with the guys in search of adventure, exploration, or even a road trip. Remember, Dad: girls like adventure, exploration, and road trips too.

When Claire was a toddler, Janelle and I would head out on various outdoor activities and take her along. Whether it were the oceans, mountains, deserts, frozen lakes, or river crossings, Claire was on the scene, and it took a road trip to get her there. We would strap her into the car seat, hand her the toy *du jour*, and hit the road. Guess what we discovered? The precocious, energetic, "What's next?" daughter we were raising, who was always on the move and didn't slow, loved the view, the adventure, and the exploration to and from the destination in the car.

The funny part of that fact is that she was good as long as the wheels were turning. Claire had a thing in her head that said, "If this car stops, we are there, and I get out." When that was not the case—due to things such as an unexpected traffic jam, the need for gas, a food stop, or a diaper change—she was not a happy camper. Janelle and I recount those memories with fond delight (and a few sighs). The adventure itself was often secondary to the games we would play with Claire to keep her mind off the realities of the road.

So when Claire was old enough, we would take a day-trip and explore something or somewhere. As she got older, we would go farther, until some of our day-trips turned into road trips—some of them taking the place of vacations. These were fun times of exploration, adventure, and bonding that are etched into our minds and recalled in pictures and videos that remain dear to our hearts.

When Claire was in junior high, and throughout her high-school years, we took small and large road trips that were separate from our family trips. These times were special in a number of ways, but at the core, it was time, sharing, and coadventure that gave me an opportunity to separate myself from competing interests (work, school, family, and schedules) to focus on her.

Though most were within the state, our last big road trip was in her junior year of high school, during Easter break. We flew into North Dakota, and over the course of a week, we drove through North Dakota, South Dakota, Montana, Wyoming, and Colorado, and we ended in the great state of Nebraska. While there, she was able to visit the home my great-great-grandfather built, see what used to be the homestead, meet relatives, retrieve a Japanese helmet from World War II that my dad originally sent home to his father, and see some additional museum articles from my family that had been donated.

It really was not about the Lewis and Clark Trail, although we followed some of it. It really wasn't about the scenery, although it is some of the best this country has to offer. And it really wasn't about the family connections, history, and wonder of Nebraska, although the trip was filled with that. It *was* about Claire. It was *all* about Claire. I had seen and done nearly all of what we experienced together over that week, but I had not done it with my daughter. That is why I did it. That is why I still take road trips with Claire.

REPAIRS

Years ago, when Claire was four or five, I took some unnecessary risks, didn't listen to Janelle, and learned a few lessons in the process. To save money, I was determined to trim a very large tree in my backyard on my own, instead of paying professionals. If I'd had the proper equipment, it might have made sense, but a Sawzall, gloves, and a six-foot fiberglass ladder did not qualify. Nevertheless, I was convinced of what I could accomplish, and so, without Janelle's blessing (but with her scowl), I began the great sapodilla tree-trimming adventure.

Emboldened by my first few successful branch cuts, I stood on the top of a six-foot fiberglass ladder—you know, the part with the big red warning sticker that says something about how "THIS IS NOT A STEP" and other legal "nonsense"—and cut an enormous branch away from the tree.

In what took only a second, the branch (which we later estimated weighed two or three hundred pounds) split just before the cutaway, pivoted, and came down, swinging like a pendulum toward me. I jumped off the top of the ladder, watching as the limb hit, snapped, and tweaked the ladder into a fiberglass catastrophe. The dust and leaves cleared to reveal something like modern museum art, more than a ladder.

Janelle and Claire, watching with interest from the kitchen window, ran outside. Janelle was not happy (which is an understatement), and Claire was just glad to see me alive and lying on the grass—and she promptly took advantage of the moment to jump on top of me and tickle me. When I got up, I surveyed the ladder, which at the time was very expensive, costing over $200.

The thought of the error of my ways, the loss of the ladder, and admitting it all to Janelle was a shot to my pride I was not willing to take. So I announced I could repair it. Janelle rolled her eyes and sarcastically blurted out to me on her way back into the house, "Yeah, you *do* that, Shad. Repair it."

I hugged Claire and retreated into the garage. Upon careful examination, I discovered a truly ingenious fix—not for my pride, but for my two-hundred-dollar ladder. The ladder leg that was snapped and fiber-frayed had been manufactured in a strength-assuming U shape. Amazingly, I had some aluminum scrap that was nearly the exact dimension. A few minutes later, I had cut the ladder leg, deburred the fiberglass, cut the aluminum channel scrap, drilled it to accept supporting nuts and bolts, and was reassembling the modern art into its original ladder form.

Janelle came out to see me testing the ladder in the yard under the tree. "You're kidding me, right? You need to trash that thing and buy another one. Admit it: it's broken," she said. However, I didn't give in. Instead, I continued. Claire came out again and surveyed the fix. She asked a lot of questions, and I answered her by explaining the concept of a splint and how, when it was complete, it would actually be even stronger than it had been before. Claire was convinced and walked away.

Finishing the repair, I wrapped the deburred cut area around the leg with electrical tape. When Claire returned, she asked why I was wrapping it. I told her it was so that we would never feel the rough-cut area or risk a fiberglass splinter. This made sense to her, and she replied, "Wait, Daddy. I have something!" as she ran off.

She returned about the time the job was complete and presented me with a stick that was about two inches long. (She used to collect small sticks, rocks, and things.) "Use this, Daddy!" I was impressed, touched, and amused. With a few additional wraps, her stick was incorporated into the splint repair of my ladder.

So many years later, the splint is still working—and so is the ladder! (And sometimes I even stand on the top when Janelle is not looking.) Claire's wood splint is still there too, reminding me that we all have a part to play in repairs.

Relationships—specifically you and your daughter's relationship—will require repair from time to time. Always be the first to suggest repair, move forward, and get things started. When it comes to the process and method of repair, don't be surprised if she comes up with her own solution. Don't assume you're the only one who knows how to get it done. In the meantime, teach her what it takes to "make things right" by being a peacemaker and a repairer of broken hearts and relationships.

Always remember how powerful your humility is in the process of repair.

Chapter 4 Recap and Checklist

☐ Building the young lady will always begin with discipline and limits.

☐ Respect is key. If your daughter does not have respect for herself, she will be incapable of respecting others. Engender respect by respecting your wife and daughter. Expect your daughter to show respect at all times. It is a principle she must live by.

☐ "Thank you" is the standard. You must communicate this essential criterion as part of your daughter's firm foundational growth. Teach her that she should be thankful all the time and in most situations.

☐ Giving her a paycheck and not an allowance will help her develop into a grateful and hard-working woman, no matter what her vocation. It is impossible for her to develop a sense of entitlement if she earns her way in life. Self-respect is at the core of this strategy.

☐ Her first date is with you. Lead her, guide her, and cherish her in the same way you want her dates to. These are deeply satisfying occasions that will have an astonishing impact on your relationship with your daughter. Set the time aside and resolve in your heart to grow, bond, and learn as you teach her.

☐ Road trips are great ways to enjoy time and adventure together. It is not about where you go or how long you're gone; it is all about your time together. Plan a trip today, Dad. The adventure awaits.

☐ Repairs are needed along the way. Fix the missteps, change course, and repair the areas you need to in order to walk in complete honesty and faithfulness in the relationship. Be a humble peacemaker in the process of repair. There is power in humility.

5

Prepuberty: Keep the Lines of Communication Open

My first-grade teacher, Mrs. Chavez, was a gifted analogist. Four-plus decades later, many of her discussions with our class of squirmy little six-year-olds have remained with me (a sign of a great teacher, to be sure). She once shared with our class the concept of communication with God and what that can look like in our minds. Allow me to restate what I recall of her analogy in my own words.

When we talk to God, as we pray, it is like two people on each end of a telephone line. At times the call is clear, and at other times it is not, but the lines of communication always remain open from His end. When there *is* a problem with the line, like when we sin or turn from Him, we won't be able to communicate effectively until the line is fixed. Sometimes repairs must take place in order to restore the valued connection we seek. In her analogy, she reminded us to always be in right relationship with the Lord. One of the best ways to do that was to stay in regular communication with Him, and if there was something wrong with the line, get it fixed. Do not delay; get up that telephone pole, and fix what is wrong with the line.

That concept also holds true for your relationship with your daughter. Sometimes you will enjoy the open and clear lines of communication with her, and the world will be at peace. Other times, through the various seasons of her life and yours, you may discover that the lines are frayed, delivering an annoying static on the line, or the lines are down, providing no possible connection. When the ebb and flow of communication with your daughter brings you to a point of limited or no communication, sound the alarm in your head and heart. When that alarm goes off, get up the pole!

Let me assure you of something, men: there is no "acceptable" amount of time that can transpire without free and clear communication with your daughter. There *is no* season where you should feel comfortable or justified in standing back or "giving her space." It is simply wrong. She needs you and your "lines" open at all times, even when she says she *doesn't* need you, doesn't hold your hand, or doesn't value your input. She still needs you and needs to know you are there.

When Claire was approaching her puberty stage, there were any number of moods, attitudes, and emotions being fired off and ricocheting off the walls of our home. It was a time that I remember like it was yesterday because I knew—all of a sudden—that this was the beginning of the "pre-puberty disconnects." I had witnessed it before in the homes of so many friends and family members. It was a period that exists within every family of girls (or *girl*, as the case may be).

It looks something like this: a girl begins to experience emotional, hormonal, and physical changes that she does not understand or is not fully equipped to handle on her own. Dad, with all of his strength, intelligence, and limited patience—also not fully equipped to handle the changes on his own—makes the first and last move in this delicate emotional chess game, setting in motion a series of responses from her that eventually further the communication decline in the relationship, sometimes for months, years, or decades.

Dad's move? He disconnects. He disconnects from her and the relationship. It's exactly the opposite of what he should do and precisely what, in his heart, he does *not* desire from these events. However, he has absolutely no understanding of how to deal with the circumstances reasonably. He is confused. He is scared (if he is honest). He may even be a little hurt. He is a man, so his first move is to show strength. This strength is displayed by action, not emotion. So he disconnects.

Men, when this season of life hits your daughter (and rocks your world and your intellect), do the opposite of what may come naturally to you. Stay. Reconnect. Share.

STAY

Guys, I don't need to give you finite examples of what *not* to do, so we'll concentrate on what *to do*. Frankly, if I gave you a "do not" case to learn from, people in my life circle would think I am speaking of their experience with their daughter. I won't do that, but that is how common this really is. The reality is that the vast majority of dads go through prepuberty relationship issues and puberty struggles with their daughters. You are not alone. So let's get busy with solutions.

Resist every urge within yourself to distance yourself from your daughter. There will be wins and losses in the game. Some pawns and other pieces may be taken off the board, but keep your king out of check. The notion that because you "don't understand what is happening" and you "can't really be helpful," or you think it is "best to leave the strategy to mom—who is the queen, of course, because she is a woman—is wrong. The truth is that your best move is to stay. When you move the king around the board, you open yourself up to checkmate. Protect the board (family), the players (each of you as individuals), and the eventual outcome of the game (your relationship) by choosing to stay.

RECONNECT

Disconnect is easy. Anyone can do that. Don't default to easy. I don't know any heroes who disconnected from those in need. Heroes stay. Heroes overcome. Heroes win, even if they are bruised and bloodied along the way. Heroes reconnect.

Have you ever noticed how special you feel when someone you love and care for deeply reconnects with you quite by surprise? Separation from our loved ones is painful. So when life's circumstances divide our attention or time spent with a loved one, but another person takes the extra step forward to reconnect, it is reassuring, comforting, and welcoming. That is exactly the response you can expect from your daughter when you reconnect during this time. If you have allowed any space to exist between you and your daughter—no matter her age—reconnect with her today. In fact, set this book down and reconnect. If you are both still breathing air, there is still time to reconnect.

SHARE

Depending upon the way you were raised and the challenges you faced in the prepuberty or puberty stages (with or without your parent's help), you may find sharing difficult. Some of you may simply refuse to share for reasons of shame, insecurity, or (in some cases) not wanting your child to consider someone else's negative experience. What may be very difficult for you as this season progresses with your daughter could be a lifesaver for her. Therefore, share.

When you got your first pimple, did you think you were the only one who had ever experienced that? Of course not. But *why* not? You didn't feel singled out or alone in that reality because you had already seen pimples. You saw them on your friends, your parents perhaps, and certainly through teen lore. You already knew that everyone deals with pimples—some more than others—during specific stages of life. You were not prepared, but you knew what was coming.

Your daughter will begin her prepubescent and puberty season believing that she is the only one who feels exactly the way she does. She will feel singled out or alone because she has not seen this before (because older teens don't mentor and share). She does not see this with her friends, her parents, or through teenage information streams. She has only heard of the "scary" physical changes, but not the emotional, irrational, and at times despondent changes that come over her unexpectedly.

Start a discussion, guys. Now, I'm not suggesting you begin with "Hey, sweetie, how's the hormone hell you're experiencing today?" Begin with the same simple conversations that brought you two together in the first place. Kick it off with something like, "Hey, sweetie, how was school?" or "Hey, I bet you have a pile of homework to do right now, but when you're finished, let's sneak out and get ice cream. I don't think I can wait for our next 'date'" or "I need a shirt for work and have to go to the mall. Wanna come with me so I get the right style and color to match my sport coat?"

Then, when you've created a simple and unassuming dialogue, you can move into something like "When I was your age, I was out of my mind with the changes. My thoughts were changing, my face was blowing up with zits, and my parents didn't have a clue, and the worst part was that I didn't think I could talk to anyone about it" and "I'm glad we have the type of relationship where you can talk to me anytime and about anything. I love that about our relationship! You rock!" Any one of those—or all of them—will elicit a response. Get ready. Listen. Love her through it.

STAYING, RECONNECTING, AND SHARING IN PRACTICE

There is an occasion that comes to mind when I consider stay, reconnect, and share. It was an event that became a pivotal juncture in my role as a dad, as a parent, and certainly as a man.

Claire was nearly ten years of age and had been exhibiting some odd, emotional, and erratic behavior with her little brother and us (but most noticeably with us). Janelle and I had considered that it was indeed a pre-puberty change occurring, but we were eager to dismiss it as "life," thinking she was too young to be experiencing prepubescent or "early puberty" symptoms. Looking back, it's comical how much we wanted to deny it to ourselves because she was *indeed* beginning to ride that hormonal roller coaster.

On this particular day, Janelle and Claire had disagreed on something earlier, Claire had been less than charitable in her interaction with Blake, and she had already mouthed off to me about something else and had been corrected. Now, from another room, I could hear Claire and Janelle arguing again, so I decided to get involved. I came into the hallway to see Janelle and Claire in the middle of it, and, like a good husband with all the best intentions, I barged into the mix and declared Claire to be wrong, out of order, and told her to apologize to Janelle and get a better attitude. (Great work, Dad. *Not*.)

Claire looked up at me, on the verge of tears, and yelled in breathless disgust, "You guys just don't get it. I'm trying to explain, but you're not listening! You guys don't listen! But I'm wrong! It's my fault, right? I'm sorry, Mom. I'm sorry, Dad. Not really, but I'm sorry." And before Janelle and I could acknowledge the flamethrower that was singeing our eyebrows, she stepped backward into her room and slammed the door—a first for her.

While I had attempted to jump in and be Janelle's support and coparent in the midst of this exhibition, when it was over, it was clear that I had in fact brought it to a boiling point and had managed to become the focus of the battle. Janelle, with characteristic maturity, poise, and class, turned to me (on my way to kick the door in), put her hand on my chest, and whispered as she stared me down, "It's official. She's in puberty. Let me handle this."

During the twenty minutes or so of talking, crying, and other noises coming from Claire's room, I calmed down, prayed, and responded to Blake's question of "What's wrong with Claire?" with "I don't know."

Then, as Janelle came out of Claire's room with a solemn and heavy look on her face while closing the door behind her, I decided to go in. Janelle stopped me again and suggested I give her some time. This time, however, I simply did not see the wisdom in that, so I knocked and entered the lion's den.

Walking into her room, I was disarmed immediately by the mere sight of her curled up on her bed, facing the wall, clutching a pile of tissues, and sniveling. I took a few more steps, sat on her bed, and asked her to sit up for a minute. She reluctantly complied, sat next to me holding the tissues, and stared at the floor. That is when it hit me like a lightning bolt, causing me to proceed with staying, reconnecting, and sharing in focus.

I reached over and took her hand. Holding it gently, I said, "Claire, I don't understand what is happening with you today or over the past few weeks, and I won't pretend to know how you are feeling inside, but I want you to hear something. When little girls get bigger, and things begin to change physically, emotionally, and in other ways, most dads run! As dads, we don't understand it. We don't know what to do about it. We don't know how to make it better. We just know we love our little girl, but she is changing, so most dads separate themselves from it. But that changes things between them, and in the end, it makes it worse for both of them. So I prayed about this and gave it a lot of thought. You are way too important to me to let you go, even for a little while. I love you way too much to distance myself from you just because I don't understand your feelings—feelings maybe you don't even understand. Our relationship is too important for me to step away and wait this out, so I won't. I want you to know that when you feel like this, or when we have a problem, I will be here and will sit with you and work it out. I want you to know that there is nothing you will do or say to me that will prevent me from sticking this out with you. I will be right here. I love you and always will, Claire!"

That was it. My uneducated, unpracticed, unvarnished, and honest one-on-one with my daughter. Her response? Total acceptance, lots of tears, a long embrace, prayer, and a new plateau in our relationship that we would have never reached without putting into practice what you read today. Stay. Reconnect. Share.

From that day forward, through her teenage years and beyond, we have never disagreed on any subject. (Ha ha ha! That was even difficult to type without laughing.) I know you don't believe that, but you can believe this: since that day, we have never allowed disagreement, emotions, or any other barrier to come between us. Even when I failed my family, disappointed my kids, or lost face with my daughter, there was always room to mend the relationship because neither one of us would allow a closure or an extended separation. That is something that defines us to this day. We are inseparable!

Chapter 5 Recap and Checklist

☐ Keep the lines of communication open. There is absolutely no acceptable amount of time that can transpire without free and clear lines of communication with your daughter. Resist the natural inclination to relax and let things take their course. Get directly involved; stay, reconnect, and share.

☐ Stay close to her emotionally during this time. Distancing yourself from a preteen is a dangerous proposition that will leave you on an island and leave her with an inclination to seek what you are not providing from someone or somewhere else.

☐ Reconnect constantly. Disconnecting is easy—especially when we (men) feel overwhelmed emotionally or don't feel as if we possess the skill set to move forward. Do not default to easy. Heroes overcome and reconnect.

☐ Share your life, your wounds, and your overcoming spirit with your daughter. When we share, we open another avenue of honesty for her to consider. This same road of honesty goes both ways. When you need her to be honest and share with you, she will.

☐ Risk it all. The relatively minor concerns of ridicule, awkward feelings, and more do not compare with the life-sustaining connection that can be found in uneducated, unpracticed, unvarnished, and honest one-on-one communication with your daughter.

6

Puberty: "Overwatch." Be There; She Needs You

In modern-day combat situations, the term *overwatch* is used to describe a protection tactic utilized to support a unit or force as they execute their mission. It is the mission of a single—often small—forward detachment or fighting vehicle tasked with the military support of an allied unit during their movement and battle engagements. This supporting unit, acting with specific overwatching intent and focus on the battle zone or active environment, holds a strategic position in order to survey the terrain ahead of the engaged unit and is particularly fixated on enemy positions. Due to its forward-thinking, proactive-oversight functions, this unit becomes a force multiplier that can surprise, suppress, and even completely overwhelm an ordinarily formidable enemy force. The advantage is in the overwatching tactic—not the size of the unit.

Dad, there may be times you'll think you're a relatively small force in the life of your daughter. Don't believe that, and don't lose sight of the enemy. There are and will continue to be a number of distractions, pitfalls, and enemy engagements that your daughter will face as she journeys from being your little princess and on through puberty, the teenage years, and adulthood. In the middle of that battleground, you are there. Yes, you're a comparatively small force in the life of your daughter when you consider outside influences and their power, but you are *her* force protection. You are *her* hero. Actively engage the enemy. Develop your overwatch strategy.

Puberty, the changes, the challenges, and the fear. Wait. Did you think I was talking about your daughter? No, this is about *you*, Dad. Puberty changes you. You go from being a dad who can scoop up your daughter, tickle her, and cuddle on the couch watching *The Princess Bride* to treating her like kryptonite for fear of overstepping the male barriers that now exist. You will be challenged by the mood swings, the physical changes, and the new daughter who sometimes is more like a house guest than your offspring. It is tough, but you can't give in or give up. Discard your fear. Get in there, and be Dad.

PURITY STILL MATTERS

This is a dark and twisted world we live in, and if you're not in full agreement with that point, just watch a few minutes of cable news or surf the Internet. Unless you're living in a bubble and do not have access to news, you know I am not sugarcoating it. Life is challenging for all of us, no matter where we live or what socioeconomic space we inhabit. Swelling within that storm is a torrent of emotions and physical changes you don't know how to handle on your own. You're getting close to how your daughter feels about life during the puberty and teenage stages of her life.

To add insult to injury, she has a media machine, social networks, peer influences, and her own curiosity regarding sex and relationships that can twist her moral compass into a question mark. Enter: Dad!

Here is where you put on your big-boy pants and get involved so that she is reminded what the moral code is and where her compass should be set. This not the time to tiptoe around the subject or leave it to your wife to handle. You can't sit this one out. You are a man—who used to be a teenage boy. This is in your wheelhouse, so steer the ship, and keep her on course!

PURITY RING—REPRESENTING A STANDARD

Like many of the strategies you will read from my life with Claire, you may modify them, skip over parts, incorporate others, or outright reject them. You are free to do any or all of them—it is *your* choice. However, I will endeavor to share what I know to be successful in the life of my daughter and what benefited her. When you consider the alternatives the world offers, these concepts do not pose a threat. They are a warm, comforting blanket that holds your precious gift secure.

Why would I preface this section with that? If you decide to guide your daughter up the higher road to purity, get ready for some social backlash. I remain shocked, dismayed, and more than a bit put off by reactions and responses I have received from some of our friends, a few within our extended family, and complete strangers who don't want me to invade their space with "morality," but they're happy to share their *lack of* it with you—and your daughter.

One example that comes to mind was from a complete stranger, who overheard the discussion I was having with the jeweler who made Claire's purity ring and his wife the day we picked up the completed ring. The wife of our jeweler was telling Claire how proud she was of her, how special the ring was, and what a great job the engraver did with the scripture references inside the ring. Just then, a woman, perhaps forty years old or so, with her maybe ten-year-old daughter in tow, leaned into our discussion and asked the jeweler's wife, "What is this ring for?" She replied that Claire and I were there to pick up her "purity ring" that they had made for her.

You would have thought someone had poured lemon juice down her throat, because all at once, she recoiled, projecting a scowl toward us, and said, "Oh. One of those religious things…I see," and she immediately took her daughter by the hand and led her away. As she walked by us, her daughter asked her what it was, and she said, "Some ring to force her not to have sex." Wow! It was a shocking event in an otherwise joyous and exciting time for Claire.

While we were shocked, we were not offended. The woman clearly was, but why? I think besides a misguided, uneducated, and misunderstood notion of what the purity ring and process are all about, she was immediately put on guard for what was a silent challenge to her and her own daughter. I could not help but wonder if this same type of person is the sort who proudly takes her daughter shopping as a preteen and teenager at the chain store, which will remain unnamed, the sole purpose of which is to sell lingerie and similar attire to young girls in preparation for a life of promiscuity and their eventual graduation into the adult-focused store next door. Tragic.

To begin, let me state that, as with other subjects and strategies I share with you in this book, this is *not* the only means by which to execute a plan to elevate and celebrate purity as a virtue and gift. Do it however you and your wife agree to. Just do it. And if you are in the unfortunate situation where your wife or ex-wife does *not* agree with the purity process and execution, do it anyway. Your daughter's understanding of what purity is and the virtue of it are insurmountable and certainly more important than your spouse's lack of clarity on the subject. Be the man. Be the dad.

When Claire turned thirteen, we had a special family meeting to present Claire's purity ring to her and to set the expectation for her, as well as to confirm our roles in the journey she would embark upon through her teenage years and beyond. The ring itself was actually designed by Claire. It was also created using gold and a stone from three rings we had in safekeeping: Janelle's "promise ring" that I had bought for her prior to our engagement, the wedding band from a very dear deceased friend of ours, and a stone from my ring.

Claire took a lot of pride in the design process and was so excited to see her ring come into reality as we met with our jeweler and discussed the steps of production. When it was complete, it was perfect. It was not what Janelle and I had pictured in our minds or how we would have designed it, but it was Claire's ring, not ours. It was her purity ring and her commitment, not ours. It was her design, her ring, and her promise that she would wear until she was married, not ours. It was uniquely Claire.

At our meeting (because *ceremony* sounds so weird, even to me), Claire, Janelle, Blake, and I stood together in our kitchen. Why the kitchen? I have no idea. To this day, I wonder, "How did we end up in the kitchen?" Well, no matter where you have your meeting, bring everyone together for it. It is a meeting that you have called, you have planned, and you will lead, but everyone in the family should take part. Your daughter needs to know that everyone is on board with this and that ultimately the family cares and looks out for each other. (Janelle also had a separate special gift for her that she used to spend extra alone time with Claire to talk through a woman's point of view.)

So we stood together as I read the following letter of presentation to her. Afterward, each of us talked and affirmed our love and concern for Claire. Blake (ten years old at the time) promised to be Claire's protector. He vowed to take an interest in any young man who desired to date her, to interview him (I'll talk more about that later), and to hold him accountable for her well-being. We ended by praying together as a family.

Claire Elizabeth Arnold
Purity Ring Presentation | 12.10.11

Claire:

This ring that I present to you today is a symbol of my deep love and concern for your physical, emotional, and spiritual well-being, and it embodies *your* sincere commitment and heartfelt dedication to stay pure before the Lord until you marry.

Your vow of purity is a deeply personal decision that represents your devotion to the Lord, obedience to his Word, acceptance and reverence for God's eternal plan for you, and loving consideration of your future husband.

As you accept this ring, you enter into a covenant with God to keep your mind, soul, and body pure from all forms of sexual sin and make a public declaration that you love God and His way— more than any sense of popularity or social acceptance.

Claire, I have selected the following scriptures for you to read, reflect, and remember through the years that precede your marriage. Each scripture reference is hand-engraved on the inside of your ring so that you may be reminded of this day, this covenant, and this LOVE that is of God's making.

God is the author of LOVE *and* intimacy. When you accept His LOVE, and respect His plan for intimacy within the boundaries of marriage, He will bless you, your spouse, your marriage, and your family. True LOVE waits! Never allow young love, passion, lust, or impatience to rob you or your spouse of the gift that is pure, true, and ordained by God.

I Corinthians 6:18
Flee from sexual immorality. All other sins a
person commits are outside the body, but whoever
sins sexually, sins against their own body.

Galatians 1:10

Am I now trying to win the approval of human beings, or of God? Or am I trying to please people? If I were still trying to please people, I would not be a servant of Christ.

I Thessalonians 4:3–8

It is God's will that you should be sanctified: that you should avoid sexual immorality; that each of you should learn to control your own body in a way that is holy and honorable, not in passionate lust like the pagans, who do not know God; and that in this matter no one should wrong or take advantage of a brother or sister. The Lord will punish all those who commit such sins, as we told you and warned you before. For God did not call us to be impure, but to live a holy life. Therefore, anyone who rejects this instruction does not reject a human being but God, the very God who gives you his Holy Spirit.

II Timothy 2:22

Flee the evil desires of youth and pursue righteousness, faith, love, and peace, along with those who call on the Lord out of a pure heart.

I love you! I am so very proud of you!
X O X O X
—Dad

SHE'LL NEED YOUR CONFIRMATION

Dad, in chapter one, we discussed the value of solid conversations with your daughter that skip over the fluff of "you're so pretty" to instead include comments that point her toward understanding how you place greater importance on her inner and expressed attributes. This is where you polish that stone. This is a time in her life and yours when you retell the story of her essential characteristics. This is when you reminisce in love over her core character, her loving heart, and her deep passion for others, and you reanchor the bonds of love that you articulated to her all those years past. Your self-assured young lady needs some reassurance, a few good hugs, and your confirmation along the way.

SHE IS UNIQUE AND SIGNIFICANT; REMIND HER

Puberty is an especially difficult time in life for girls. For reasons you do and don't understand, it will change things about your daughter. It will change her outlook on enormously complex areas of life, such as peer relationships, faith, family, friends, sex, and more. This all happens while she rides a hormonal and emotional roller coaster she didn't board willingly and wouldn't mind getting off now. Some changes will be perceptible immediately, but others will incubate in her heart, mind, and attitude over time. This critical stage in her life, as with few other occasions or settings, will afford you an exceptionally well received—and desperately needed—reminder. She is unique. She is significant.

It doesn't take big gifts or immense thought or planning. Just be there. Simply remind her of her significance in your own special way. Janelle has always done such a great job with this with both of our kids, placing sticky notes in their lunches or inside their schoolbooks. For me, I enjoyed leaving notes under their pillows, sending a text, or telling the kids, "I could really use a hug." This first move comes back to you in spades, because when you admit your need, they are more willing to do the same. It was not unusual for our kids to emerge from hours of homework and come to Janelle or me to declare, "I need a hug." That's when you deliver the reminder, the support, the uplifting message that she is unique and significant—and how proud you are of her.

Since their first day of school, I have always hugged and kissed the kids on the cheek and told them I loved them as they left for school or when I left for work. Some parents let that slide a bit and eventually let it go completely once their kids are in this stage of life. Teenagers don't want mushy, embarrassing expressions of love at that age. Right?

No. That is *so* wrong. Don't let that go, Dad. Be the man, the hero, the support, and the dad who loves his daughter and is not afraid to keep showing it to her throughout those uncertain years. In public and in private, let her know you love her with appropriate physical expressions of your love and care.

DRESS FOR SUCCESS

For years, we've heard the axioms "Dress for success," "The suit makes the man," and "The dress makes the woman." What about your daughter? How does she dress? Take a moment to consider something that society has chosen to forget. The way your daughter dresses—or, should I say, is permitted by you and your wife to dress—has a direct impact and correlation to how she will be thought of and treated by adults, fellow teenagers, and especially boys and men.

I don't think it is my place to identify exactly what your daughter should wear, but as a man, you should know exactly what she *shouldn't* wear! You are a man. You know what makes you and teenage boys "tick." You know what boys and men think about all the time. You know what clothing—or lack thereof—makes boys consider something other than wholesome thoughts and math homework. If what your daughter wears does not matter to you, it should.

How a preteen or teenage girl dresses affects the way she feels about herself, the decisions she will make, and the assumptions boys will make about her. If your daughter wears clothing that focuses on her sexuality—or clothing that displays sexuality motivated or suggestive words or phrases—there is only one conclusion boys and men will arrive at: she is promiscuous.

Society at large and the billions of dollars spent on advertising prefer promiscuity over purity. There is no revelation there, but what uninhibited behavior or dress code do *you* allow to emanate from your own home? What is your preference? Do you prefer purity or promiscuity for your daughter? Do you prefer that your daughter be objectified by society in her manner of dress or acclaimed for good works that changed lives?

Would you prefer that your daughter shop at the teen lingerie store, learning how to become a sexual object before she is even an adult or can understand the full import and lasting realities of sexual activity? Would it make you proud and content as a father to realize your daughter has chosen to seek attention not for her inner beauty, intelligence, and human worth but for her body, the control that promiscuous behavior or tease has over boys and men, or be the envy of other girls? Would you prefer that the boys and perverted men who may see your daughter objectify her, classify her, and assume something that is perhaps *not* true of her based solely on her attire?

Here is the tragedy with what we see today: moms across America and around the world are doing far more than acquiescing to a misguided path and dress decisions of a teenage daughter. By allowing them to dress provocatively, it has moved far beyond consenting or acceptance. Too often, the mother is the instigator, the gateway, and the financier of these foolish decisions. The mom is largely the one shopping with, approving of, and purchasing the items. I will go so far as to say that some more extreme mothers, emboldened in their strange quest to live vicariously through their young daughters, have in effect (just like a madam) walked their own daughters up to the door of promiscuity, opened it, and pushed them over the threshold.

Do you or your wife disagree? If so, I ask you (and anyone who would disagree with me on this point) a few questions: Would you, as man and father, feel comfortable walking into these stores with your daughter, picking out see-through bras for her, sizing revealing lingerie outfits, and watching her try on skintight so-called exercise pants and tops that would have been considered soft porn just ten years ago if worn in public?

Now, what about the people around you in the store? Would those same people approve of your fatherly presence in the store? What problem would you (or those looking on) have with your involvement? Could it be the fact that you are a man, a father, shopping with your teenage daughter for sexy or revealing outfits that belong in a bedroom between adults? Ironic, isn't it? If it is wrong for you to be there in such a clearly inappropriate situation with your daughter, why is it not equally wrong, absurd, and revolting that a mother would be doing the same?

Dad, for a moment, set aside the natural male instinct you have for the opposite sex. Separate your inclination toward alluring, sexually suggestive, or lust-filled images of women in lingerie, bras, and the like. Ask yourself a few questions: As a father, would you want to know that any of the women or young girls in the images of advertisements, four-by-six-foot blown-up versions of the same in the storefront, massive eight-by-ten-foot wall varieties, or even the billboard hanging over the freeway is *your* daughter? Would you be okay with the idea of *your* daughter (along with millions of other young women starving for attention) entering these stores and paying to be devalued? Yes. I said *devalued*. They are paying to be devalued.

In this so-called enlightened society where women's rights and equality are acknowledged and celebrated, we have lost sight of the fact that this soft porn of sorts that we allow in the public space of our malls, magazines, and television commercials is devaluing women. So much worse than that, it is *now* devaluing young girls! It is a very profitable flesh game to the global market of these types of stores. How far can we push the envelope of marketing? How far can we move the line of decency before we get in trouble?

Is there another living human being on this planet (who is not already involved in the pornography industry or the growing teenage lingerie market) who does not believe that the public display of society's daughters will lead us further down a slide that devalues women?

I am not an anthropologist, nor do I hold degrees in the social sciences, advanced analysis of social evolution, or the global implications of modern cultural transitions. I *do*, however, hold to the standards of purity, decency, and a basic respect for women. My firmly held Christian faith and beliefs aside, I fail to see the connection between the socially acceptable wholesale flesh offering of young girls and women in the malls of America and beyond, especially along with women's rights and universal respect. It is actually more akin to slavery, the flesh trade, and voyeurism.

I offer a grave prediction for America. Within a few years—perhaps ten or less—we will witness the attempt (and likely success) of the same people who support and profit from this trade pushing a new agenda. I believe their next move will be to lower the age of consent. They will propose and lobby to an increasingly liberal and tolerant electorate that our current standards for consent are bordering on archaic. They will suggest that we live in extraordinary times of intellect, scientific discovery (which they'll define in terms of cell phone and social-media technologies—not real science), and broad understanding of the human psyche. They will press on with the idea that the teenager of *today* is so far beyond her predecessors, and her consideration of such things as sexual consent is at a mature level, and she is thus legally competent to engage in such activity at a younger age.

After all, if a teenager in America can obtain a legal abortion without the consent of the parent, why wouldn't that same society vote to lower the age of consent to match the age of that same teen girl? It stands to reason that the same abortion organizations and clinics that harvest and sell the eviscerated parts of fetuses will need more in the future to ensure a profitable growth. A good steady supply of impregnated and desperate teen girls is a good bet on the commodities-and-futures market. Yes, I think it is safe to assume that those same organizations will promote the lowering of the age of consent.

My guess is they will start with a new age-of-consent proposal of sixteen years of age. There are more than enough *enlightened* senators and congressmen who will jump onto that slide. A few years later, that will indeed seem too restrictive, outdated, and imperious, and they will call for a suitable change again.

Dad, it is time to battle the popular, push back the socially acceptable, and stand for something: your daughter. Men, it is time to communicate with your wife, ex, or whoever is the shopping partner of your daughter. It is time to put your foot down and make it clear to everyone that your daughter will not be the next object of desire, teenage tool of marketing, or victim of crime or lust that begins with her clothing choices. Your daughter will have a lifetime to dress provocatively for her husband. She can shop at the lingerie store then. She shouldn't be shopping the teen version of the same store now, and her mom should *not* be the chauffeur to it or to any other store that objectifies young girls or teens or that devalues women.

OTHER THOUGHTS AND IDEAS TO CONSIDER

No matter how "cool" you think you are and how accepting of you and your ideas you *think* your kids are (specifically your daughter), most teenagers simply tolerate their parents' ideas of a great time spent together and suffer through all sorts of family events and obligations, until one day they realize those events actually *were* better than tolerable. They will see that those events molded their concept of family life and served to engender warm and fond feelings of their time at home growing up. Having said that, planning special events with your daughter or bringing her in on a surprise for someone she is close to is an outstanding technique that can bolster your relationship and open additional avenues for communication, comradery, and shared passions.

Two of these types of instances that come to my mind were tied to my twentieth wedding anniversary. Claire was twelve years old and could keep a secret, so on one of our daddy-daughter dates, I filled her in on the broad strokes of my strategy. I told her I was planning two special surprises for Janelle while we were on vacation in Hawaii (a month before our anniversary so she wouldn't be suspecting anything).

I told Claire that even though Janelle thought we were using our airline miles and hotel points to be able to simply afford the trip to Hawaii, I had actually been earning some additional side money as well as saving a little bit every month from our budget for nearly two years in order to design, build, and pay for a new wedding ring! In addition, I was in the initial planning stages of making arrangements for Janelle and me to renew our vows on a white sandy beach with palm trees and a rainbow in the background. (Full disclosure: I didn't plan on the rainbow, but Claire and I joked about it so much that I think the Lord decided it would be cool too, so we *did* have a sweet rainbow in the background of our photos and video.)

Claire was extraordinarily excited about the whole thing. For six months or so, we would have clandestine meetings and share surreptitious giggles over the secret, the plan, and the fun it was creating within our relationship. We would visit the jeweler to discuss and talk about the details of the ring and make payments accordingly. We would covertly share updates and strategies for the renewal ceremony. It was great. It was fun. It was something special that she was clued in on that Mom didn't know a thing about. A side benefit was that she got to see how a man, a husband, and a dad treats his wife; honors their marriage; and extends the extra effort to grow *that* relationship.

When I reminisce about the afternoon we sprang the surprise on Janelle—the limo ride to the beach, the renewal ceremony, the new ring, and the entire evening over dinner—I believe Claire was actually smiling wider than Janelle and I combined. She had partnered with me from inception to completion. She had experienced and co-witnessed the love, emotion, and joy of it all—and she was an integral part of each step. It was something special that we did together, and we both knew it was incomparable.

The takeaway here, men, is that you should look for areas and opportunities to demonstrate the value of (and build up) her essential characteristics. Showing love, care, and concern for others—no matter who they are—and doing special things to express that sentiment is a branch of her core character that you want to water, maintain, and then witness it bearing fruit in due season. It is *not* about a ring, a celebration, or a "thing." This is about teaching her to step outside herself to see others.

Chapter 6 Recap and Checklist

☐ Puberty is a time when you must tune in and stay involved. "Overwatch" is your new modus operandi. It is tough, but you can't give in or give up. Discard your fear. Get in there, and be Dad.

☐ Purity still matters. You can't sit this one out. You are a man—who used to be a teenage boy. This is in your wheelhouse, so steer the ship and keep her on course!

☐ The purity ring represents a standard. A purity ring is *not* the only means by which to execute a plan to elevate and celebrate purity as a virtue and gift. Whatever you and your wife decide to do, just do it.

☐ She'll need your confirmation. This is a time in her life and yours when you retell the story of her essential characteristics.

☐ She is unique and significant. Remind her of all the reasons she is special, valuable, and loved. Don't let this time in her life escape without connecting, expressing your love, and showing concern.

☐ Your daughter should dress for success. How a preteen and teenage girl dresses affects the way she feels about herself, the decisions she will make, and the assumptions boys will make about her. Allowing your daughter to wear alluring or suggestive clothing devalues her in society and plays into the marketing of flesh that retailers benefit from.

☐ Plan and experience a special occasion or event with your daughter. Use that time and the impact of it to demonstrate love to someone else together. This will be an incomparable and special time in life that she will remember with you for a lifetime.

7

Teenage Years: Hold Fast, and Lock It Down (It's Going to Get Nautical)

The dreaded teenage years…I wonder how many of you picked up this book and turned immediately to this chapter. I would have. It's true that the teenage years are challenging, but I want to give you hope and encouragement in this time. It is only a season. Just like a bitter winter storm, it will not last. The warm days of summer will return before you know it. The infamous teenage years do not have to be a nightmare in your memory or hers. In fact, they can be not only an honest reflection of good and bad, happy and sad but also a refining season that you both grow from.

HOLD FAST

I've always loved the bold and demanding statement "hold fast." Definition sources claim its origin traces back to sailing times of the Norsemen or the Dutch when sailors had to "hold fast" to the ship's rigging in rough seas. But in fact, its call to hold on tightly to something goes back to Biblical times with references to faith, hope, and the truth of God's Word. You don't have to be a Christian to acknowledge the historical proofs and truths of the Bible. In our Bible, there are at least twenty-four references to "hold fast" or "stand fast." For reference, I have included them here (my emphasis added).

You shall fear the Lord your God; you shall serve Him, and to Him you shall *hold fast*, and take oaths in His name. (Deut. 10:20)

76

For if you carefully keep all these commandments which I command you to do—to love the Lord your God, to walk in all His ways, and to *hold fast* to Him. (Deut. 11:22)

You shall walk after the Lord your God and fear Him, and keep His commandments and obey His voice; you shall serve Him and *hold fast* to Him. (Deut. 13:4)

But take careful heed to do the commandment and the law which Moses the servant of the Lord commanded you, to love the Lord your God, to walk in all His ways, to keep His commandments, to *hold fast* to Him, and to serve Him with all your heart and with all your soul. (Josh. 22:5)

but you shall *hold fast* to the Lord your God, as you have done to this day. (Josh. 23:8)

But Elisha was sitting in his house, and the elders were sitting with him. And the king sent a man ahead of him, but before the messenger came to him, he said to the elders, "Do you see how this son of a murderer has sent someone to take away my head? Look, when the messenger comes, shut the door, and *hold* him *fast* at the door. Is not the sound of his master's feet behind him?" (2 Kings 6:32)

Then the Lord said to Satan, "Have you considered My servant Job, that there is none like him on the earth, a blameless and upright man, one who fears God and shuns evil? And still he *holds fast* to his integrity, although you incited Me against him, to destroy him without cause." (Job 2:3)

Then his wife said to him, "Do you still *hold fast* to your integrity? Curse God and die!" (Job 2:9)

He leans on his house, but it does not stand. He
holds it *fast*, but it does not endure. (Job 8:15)

My righteousness I *hold fast*, and will not let it go; My
heart shall not reproach me as long as I live. (Job 27:6)

For thus says the Lord: "To the eunuchs who keep My Sabbaths,
And choose what pleases Me, and *hold fast* My covenant. (Isa. 56:4)

Also the sons of the foreigner Who join themselves to the
Lord, to serve Him, And to love the name of the Lord,
to be His servants—Everyone who keeps from defiling
the Sabbath, And *holds fast* My covenant. (Isa. 56:6)

Why has this people slidden back, Jerusalem,
in a perpetual backsliding? They *hold fast* to
deceit, They refuse to return. (Jer. 8:5)

by which also you are saved, if you *hold fast* that word which I
preached to you—unless you believed in vain. (1 Cor. 15:2)

*hold*ing *fast* the word of life, so that I may
rejoice in the day of Christ that I have not run
in vain or labored in vain. (Phil. 2:16)

and not *hold*ing *fast* to the Head, from whom all the body,
nourished and knit together by joints and ligaments,
grows with the increase that is from God. (Col. 2:19)

Test all things; *hold fast* what is good. (1 Thess. 5:21)

Therefore, brethren, *stand fast* and hold the traditions which you
were taught, whether by word or our epistle. (2 Thess. 2:15)

Hold fast the pattern of sound words which you have heard from
me, in faith and love which are in Christ Jesus. (2 Tim. 1:13)

*hold*ing *fast* the faithful word as he has been taught,
that he may be able, by sound doctrine, both to exhort
and convict those who contradict. (Titus 1:9)

but Christ as a Son over His own house, whose
house we are if we *hold fast* the confidence and the
rejoicing of the hope firm to the end. (Heb. 3:6)

Seeing then that we have a great High Priest who
has passed through the heavens, Jesus the Son of
God, let us *hold fast* our confession. (Heb. 4:14)

Let us *hold fast* the confession of our hope without
wavering, for He who promised is faithful. (Heb. 10:23)

I know your works, and where you dwell, where Satan's throne
is. And you *hold fast* to My name, and did not deny My faith
even in the days in which Antipas was My faithful martyr,
who was killed among you, where Satan dwells. (Rev. 2:13)

Woodworkers use a bench or table lock called a holdfast that can secure
irregularly shaped or flat pieces of wood to the worker's bench. Likewise,
blacksmiths cannot work effectively without this device, as it holds small or
cumbersome pieces securely. Marine biologists recognize the name "holdfast" as a reference to a fibrous edifice that anchors aquatic sessile organ-
isms to a surface with a rootlike structure. Castles and fortresses have long
since been referred to as *holdfasts* because they do exactly what the term
implied—hold fast that position, claim the land, and not let it go.

One of my top ten movies of all times, *Master and Commander*, has, in
a pointed scene in the movie, an old, weathered, and wounded sailor whose

hands are clenched into fists as he undergoes brain surgery while in a comatose state. Tattooed on his knuckles are "H-O-L-D F-A-S-T." So, indeed, it carries its demand through history and into movies and common folklore.

The concept when applied to your daughter is to hold on to her tightly. Don't let her go. When the storm of the teenage years hits your family's ship, you must retain the grasp you have on her and hold on to the foundations you've put in place to see you through. Hold on to the rigging that you fixed to the deck and masts years before. Hold the position. Be her dad.

Remind her that changes, challenges, and frustration are felt by all, but acknowledge her unique space and circumstances along the way. Perhaps one of the worst pep talks you can give your daughter contains phrases such as *Everybody goes through that, Get over it; I felt the same way,* or *You're making too much of this.* I certainly don't support a fake, pseudo-supportive, or coddling behavior by parents toward their teens. That is wrong on many levels. But you can't run to the other side of the field and diminish your daughter's personal experience in your attempt for her to "move on."

The fact is, if you're present, aware, and connected, there will be many times in your daughter's teen years that you will need to sit with her, stop the world from spinning for a few moments, recognize her dilemma, hear her defeated soul cry out, and allow her to share her admittedly limited perspective on a subject or problem she is struggling with.

It might be a friend or foe relational issue, a school-related theme, or just life. Whatever it is, you need to stop, listen, and allow her expression to be exercised so that she remembers you are her safe harbor and a safe person to open up to. Remember, men, she is going to open up to someone—better you than ill-equipped friends, social-media input, or worse yet, a predator trolling the Internet looking for lost girls.

LOCK IT DOWN; IT'S GOING TO GET NAUTICAL

The teenage years are here, and you're doing your best, but it's getting windy. The whitecaps are everywhere, the swells are rising and rocking your ship back and forth, and the rigging, along with your precious cargo, are swaying and threatening to break loose. What will be the outcome of this storm you're caught in? Lock it down!

We can read, in thousands of historical records, accounts of ships who were held within the grasp of a storm, facing certain disaster. To save the ship and the souls aboard, they would throw the ballasts, the anchor, and even the cargo overboard. Have you considered that in your life? When the storm and gales rage on during those fragile years, what will you discard to save her? What will you give up to hold her character, her mind, her emotions, her faith, and her very life in safe harbor?

Don't lean in too quickly to protest and claim that it either won't happen to you or your family dynamics won't be distressed and strained during these times—or that when it does, you won't be willing to do anything at all to save her. Examine your life, your walk, your commitments, and your leisure activities. Are you an executive, a traveler, a golfer, a socially connected hipster? Whatever you are and whichever category you place yourself in, if you are engaged in anything other than the standard "go to work and come home each evening to your family" sort of life, you can expect some disruption of your schedule. Be willing now to commit to changing your reality to positively affect hers.

It pains me to share that more than one of my friends, colleagues, and many others whom I only know of from a distance lost it all. They went into the storm prepared but failed to hold fast. They didn't lock it down, and at the last possible moment, they flinched, failing to cast other "important" things in their lives overboard, and they watched their ship go down—all souls lost. Too melodramatic? Too exaggerated? Perhaps a little over the top? No. Men fail at this. There is no sugarcoating it. Dump what does not matter, and dig deep with your daughter.

Here's a final thought. Living in Orange County, our family has experienced a number of small, medium, and large wildfires in and around the communities we've lived in. Most of the time, they are caused by careless smokers who toss their cigarettes out the window instead of depositing them in their own ashtrays. Worse cases are the evil and malicious acts of the arsonists who live among us in society. When the fire is raging, and the

Santa Ana winds are blowing their fiery embers into neighboring communities, we concern ourselves with *what* we need to do now—not so much with *how* we do what needs to be done. In our case, we have had the unenviable task of calling a family meeting to pray—and then packing what *really* matters into our vehicles and preparing to evacuate.

It is a surreal feeling, but as I have shared with others who have not experienced it, the lack of control is a uniquely centering exercise, a special moment in time not to be enjoyed but certainly one that can be appreciated. At the core of the decisions made in those few moments is a prevailing thought, demand, and question: "What matters most to me right now and could not be replaced?" The obvious things go in the vehicles first: family, pets, pictures, records, art, and so on. Then comes the secondary list: some clothes, toiletries, laptops, and the like. Lastly is the final list, to which we say, "Forget it! There is no more room in the SUV, and there is no more time. Evacuate now!"

Until you've been subjected to that experience, you will not know the power it has over you. However, when you come out of it, you are stronger. You know what *really* matters. So, if you would acknowledge and even agree that your choices in that case would be quite similar—if not exactly the same—then imagine what you would do if your daughter's life and your family unit (your ship) is on fire? What would you be willing to get rid of, leave behind, and walk away from in order to make a difference and keep your daughter safe? Would you move your career, your hobbies, your dreams, and more to the secondary or final list that may not come back to you? Would you set down your plans and your ideal picture of what these years *should* be like in order to make a difference in your daughter's life? Men around you will directly or indirectly choose *their* lives, *their* careers, *their* golf games, or *their* other vices over their daughter. Be different. Be Dad.

WHEN YOU FAIL—BECAUSE YOU WILL

As a father, a husband, and a man, I fail. I say "I fail" rather than "I have failed" because the sad fact is that I fail in big and small ways all the time. Most of the time, no one is around to point it out, but it is still a failure whether someone else sees it or not. You wouldn't want to buy this book, much less read it, if I listed all my "dad failings" in order. That said, I believe in the importance of continuing to cultivate trust with you, the reader, since a number of my suggestions and ideas are prescriptive. In this segment, I reluctantly share a terrible failure of mine that began with my daughter and affected my whole family.

Some time ago, on Easter of all days, I failed my daughter, my son, and my wife. The background—while certainly not an excuse—includes a few extenuating factors that contributed to my bankrupt response to an issue with Claire. Some weeks earlier, I was prescribed a new medication for osteoarthritis pain that was making me quite irritable, but I stayed on it because it alleviated the daily pain. Only three days before, while meeting with a men's group that I am a part of at our church, I shared some very difficult facts about my childhood that I had not previously shared with anyone other than Janelle. The discussion and the memories of what I presented sat with me for days, and instead of it being a "freeing" experience, it filled me with anxiety and pulled me into a state of depression, which led to anger. The day before, Janelle and I had dealt with some extended-family issues and drama related to the Easter holiday. That day, our plans for Easter dinner would be canceled because of my elderly father's illness. All in all, the pump of frustration and irritation was primed; I was ready to blow.

I have thought about the details, the moments before, and the words said—or yelled—during the argument with Claire and then with Janelle. I had typed them out to include here, but then I held down the backspace key. The reasons, the words, and the gritty details do not really matter. What matters is this: I completely lost my mind, heart, and soul for my daughter, my wife, and my son in an inexcusable fit of rage and anger that I had not experienced or expressed since I was a lost and wandering teen decades ago. I reacted to a perceived level of disrespect, a disregard for my role as the father, in what felt like "one more thing" going wrong and one more out-of-my-control situation in life. Within minutes, I had accused; yelled; disparaged; cursed; and, like a petulant child; thrown a fit-to-be-tied tirade that blamed everyone but myself. I was absolutely out of control—and immediately ashamed.

My family was in complete shock. I had never been angry like this. I had never reacted to anything like I did at that moment. I had never failed with such explosive exhibition. I had lost their respect and failed so deeply, all in a matter of seconds. Grabbing my car keys, I got in my car and drove.

HUMILITY, CONFESSION, APOLOGIES: THE ROCK-SOLID PROOF YOU'RE *REAL* AND NOT A HYPOCRITE

A few hours later, I returned and gave the following letter to my family. I put it at the door to each of their rooms and left the house again. I needed space, time, and forgiveness. An "all clear" was not going to come quickly.

> *Dear Family,*
>
> *I am humiliated by my own reckless, angry, and regrettable loss of control.*
>
> *Please forgive me and know that my actions are my fault, my responsibility, and my shame to bear.*
>
> *I am so very sorry for allowing my response to problems to become greater than Jesus and His Holy Spirit in my life today—of all days.*
>
> *It is a horrible example of everything that I have promised myself never to be to my family. Forgive me.*
> *You are loved. I am sorry.*

Just reading those words again reminds me of something that is so very painful, embarrassing, and utterly humiliating. *That is* what happened, so I have to own it. I'd love to omit this entire story from this book (you'd never know), but I can't. It happened, and I have grown through it. Maybe you are a dad who has failed miserably too. Humble yourself before God and your family, confess it, and apologize. That will be their proof that you are not a hypocrite.

The next day I called the family together and apologized again. I spent time with each family member privately to express my continued sorrow and contrition and to reassure each of them that he or she is my life, my love, and my greatest hope and dream fulfilled. It took time, but we came back together as a family and individually, because we all have learned to forgive as we ourselves have been forgiven. I am thankful for that and for them.

From chaos can come breakthrough. That pathetic event led me to write a lengthy letter—practically a treatise—to my children that Janelle read and agreed they should receive from me someday in the future when it's right. In it, I share with them some of the devastation and pain in my childhood that I had held in for over forty years, the anger that I have always bottled up, and the release that I only now have because I have chosen to forgive—as I have been forgiven—and move on.

Men, this is a critical point to grasp. I am a failed, flawed, and imperfect man. I always will be. What I choose to do with that reality depends upon me. In your case, it is entirely up to you. Like me and every other father, you will fail. Will it be private or public? Will you be courageous by being contrite and displaying humility? Will you confess and apologize? Will you be the dad you wish *you'd* had growing up? Will you be a hypocrite or a flawed example of a *real* man and a *real* dad?

SPRINKLES MAKE IT BETTER

After saying all of that, I could use a few sprinkles!

I discovered (quite by accident), that sprinkles (the colorful cupcake and dessert topping) make it better—no matter what "it" is.

When Claire was nearing two years of age, she tripped and fell on our back patio while playing with our little dogs. She had a very minor scrape on her knee and the palm of her left hand. She came in with Janelle through the back door, which was at the opposite end of our galley-style kitchen, and she stood there screaming and crying. As I made my way through the kitchen to her, she looked up at me as if to say, "This is the end, Daddy. It doesn't get any worse than this." Meanwhile, Janelle signed and mouthed to me that she would go get the antibacterial solution and some Band-Aids.

I knelt down to give Claire a reassuring hug, hold her, and attempt to calm her frantic spirit, knowing the worst of it was actually on its way in Janelle's hands (why do antibacterial solutions sting so badly?). When the initial round of comfort faded, and her screams and sobs diluted into snivels and drip-drop tears, I looked up from my kneeling position and noticed the small glass shaker of cupcake sprinkles sitting on the counter. Suddenly, it hit me: sprinkles are colorful, magical, and could surely make anything better. After all, they are processed sugar.

I wiped Claire's tears from her face and said, "Claire, I think you're old enough to learn a secret. Can I share a very special secret with you?"

Looking into my eyes, with a sniff and a quick clearing of her throat, she said, "Yes, Daddy."

I proceeded to share with her that, besides being applied to cakes and cupcakes, sprinkles actually have special power. If you eat one or two, maybe three for really bad stuff, they can "make it all better." Then I asked, "Would you like me to give you some sprinkles?"

It was a fifty-fifty shot. She was a smart one, and it was always quite difficult to pull anything over on her. Would she call me on it or go along and discover the "special power" of sprinkles?

As she considered my assertion, she stood up from my side, wiped her face and bangs, looked at me, and said, "Yes please, Daddy." I reached up on the counter, retrieved the clear glass dispenser filled with colorful sprinkles, and shook out three into my hand, prompting her to take one at a time and tell me if it worked. With that, she reached slowly toward each one, taking care to insert each one onto her tongue like a communion wafer and savor its magical properties. After the third one was completely gone, she said, "Thank you, Daddy! I'm better now."

That scenario wove itself in and out of her toddler and young-lady years when things got tough. Even as a two-year-old, after the second or third time, she knew that this "magic properties" stuff was a bunch of hooey. However, she was not going to let on to me that she knew it because she got a few sugary sprinkles out of the deal.

Over the years, sprinkles became more of a touchstone of concern, love, and caring than magical bits of processed sugar that could take away pain. Whether she was feeling overwhelmed with homework, AP class assignments, or honors math, sprinkles could come to the rescue, representing my concern and care. When hot chocolate with whipped cream and sprinkles shows up on your desk at 9:45 p.m., it means something. When a warm slice of banana bread and a few out-of-place sprinkles on a plate appear on your history book, it says something.

When Claire went off to college and became strained with the understandable away-from-home, distant (electronic-only) connection to family, and the resulting sadness and lonely feelings, I ordered a variety pack of sprinkles from Amazon and shipped them up to her with a gift note. It was *very* well received! One of us even shed a few tears over it all. I'll let you guess who that was.

Chapter 7 Recap and Checklist

☐ "Hold fast" is the requirement during this tumultuous time, Dad. Hold fast to your daughter. Remind her that changes, challenges, and frustrations are felt by all—but acknowledge her unique space and circumstances along the way.

☐ Lock it down. Work, leisure, family, and more will be disrupted during this time, so lock it down and decide what really matters. Be willing to commit to changes that positively affect your daughter's reality.

☐ Men around you will choose *their* lives, *their* careers, *their* golf games, or other vices—directly or indirectly—over their daughters. Be different. Be Dad.

☐ When you fail—because you will—be humble, confess, and apologize. From the chaos can come breakthroughs, so be prepared to be a flawed example of a real man, a real dad. That is always better than being a hypocrite.

☐ Sprinkles make it better, so use them accordingly. Develop something special between you and your daughter that can be a touchstone during tough times.

8

Dating: Locked and Loaded

Over the years, Claire and Blake have shared with me fascinating little anecdotes about their friends who, for some reason, have characterized me as very intimidating upon initially meeting me. For some this thought did not go away for years. In fact, one of Claire's best friends, her sister, and subsequently her parents came to suspect that I was in the CIA, FBI, or some other deep clandestine organization—an idea that was confirmed in their minds by the fact that I have traveled to a number of "closed" countries.

When I would hear about this, I would laugh aloud, until one day my son said, "Seriously, Dad. I mean this. Your sunglasses, your size, your look, and your commanding presence can all be intimidating when you're on campus—especially when you don't say much!"

Full disclosure: I am not in the CIA, FBI, or some other deep clandestine organization—to which those same friends of Claire would exclaim, "That's exactly what you would say if you were!" In fact, my foreign travel to what might be described as closed or difficult countries is tied to my volunteer work with Novitas Foundation in its humanitarian efforts for children around the world. I am, however, always conscious of how I present myself to others, especially Blake and Claire's friends and acquaintances.

It has long been my focused goal and strategy as their father to be a physical and psychological impediment to any folly and nefarious activity. So, in that respect, I suppose it has been a successful undertaking. I don't mind that Claire and Blake have schoolmates, dates, or hangers-on who consider me an intimidating guy. Good! After all, if they knew that I was in fact a loving, caring, gentle, and nurturing father—and great host and friendly sort to their friends and guests in our home who loves to cook and produce culinary creations for them and who enjoys having them over and doing things with them—then the unsavory types that float in and out of all of our children's lives might consider it an opportunity to take advantage of. I like the way it has turned out, and so do my kids.

When I speak of being a "physical and psychological impediment to any folly and nefarious activity," you might suspect that I am principally referring to boys, prospective dates, and the like. You would be correct. It is my job as Claire's dad to instill a healthy—or unhealthy, as the case may be—balance of intimidation, uncertainty, and questionable psychosis in the hearts and minds of a prospective date. Threats are illegal in most states and frankly "old school," so I do not ascribe to them. Mind games are so much more useful and satisfying in the end. (No wonder our kids' friends think I'm in the CIA.)

I'll bet you thought I meant something else when I entitled this chapter "Dating: Locked and Loaded." Did you *think* there was an implication to that? Hmm.

THE INTERVIEW

We discussed respect in depth in chapter 4. Now is the time when the respect you engendered in the early years pays dividends for both you and your daughter. It goes without saying that when she learns to respect others, she will grow to respect herself. When she respects herself, she will absolutely recoil and emphatically reject any level of disrespect from a boy or date; she simply won't tolerate it. That is the key. You aren't going to be there in the car with her on a date (don't even consider it, Dad) or in the theater or at the school dance. You'll have to rely on her self-respect to keep her out of trouble. We'll deal with her date's self-respect in a moment.

Claire was nearing sixteen when she went on her first date. We had communicated to her for many years that she would be allowed to date at eighteen, but that was always a ploy to extend the process and keep boys away until she was mature enough to date (in her case, it was when she was nearly sixteen). At whatever age you allow your daughter to date (and that is relative to her maturity and your wisdom—not anyone's book), do *not* permit it without expectations (and certainly don't plan for it the day of). Get ready now, and put a plan in place. There is a lot of "input" you can read out there that you may or may not want to consider, but I'll share what we did in Claire's situation.

With Claire, dating happened after presenting her the purity ring, but most importantly, it was once Janelle and I agreed she was mature enough. It did not begin without interviews. Yes. That's "interviews" in the plural sense. Claire has a brother. Though he is almost three years younger, he is her brother, and we gave him permission (as did Claire) to be a part of the interview process years before her first date. You might expect some blustering from your daughter on sibling input, but if she is anything like Claire, she will actually appreciate it.

If you are unfamiliar with the procedure, it looks something like this. A young man asks Claire if she would like to go out on a date, attend an event, or go to some function where they are alone, as in a "one-on-one date." Claire informs said young man (assuming she would like to) that she would like that very much, but he'll need to meet with and interview with her father and brother beforehand.

At this point, if the young man has *any* class and a modicum of respect for her, he agrees and immediately understands how important Claire is to her father and brother. Additionally, if he has matured beyond the common societal norms, he is actually impressed and begins to feel all the more interested in Claire because she must be a very special gift worth protecting. If not, bye-bye!

Don't gloss over that, Dad. You and I were both teenagers (so many years ago), and we both know what young men think about *all day long*. We know that no matter what your daughter's upbringing is or was, she is vulnerable. No matter what her date's upbringing is or was, he is also vulnerable. He is susceptible to temptation, immature decision-making, and who knows what else with your daughter, some or all of which could have lasting or lifelong consequences.

Let's go back a bit. When you brand yourself "a physical and psychological impediment to any folly and nefarious activity," the young man will know there is something very different about you, your daughter, and her brother(s) (if she has any). You will be occupying valuable space in his head before you ever meet! Get it? I assure you, he certainly will.

It has a dual effect as well. He will likely share your "interview first" policy with his parents. Their response could be good or bad; I've found there is no in-between. The parents who like it may actually contact you and thank you (it's happened to me). The other side of that coin is that you may have parents who contact you to ask you why. Don't spend too much time explaining. They disagreed before you ever formed a response. They might tolerate it, but they will not support it, and they will assume their son is being threatened, intimidated, or brainwashed. Just be prepared. And remember, she is *your* daughter—not theirs!

At this point, Claire would come home and let Janelle and me know that she had been asked out on a date. We would talk about the young man and her thoughts and feelings about him, and if everything jived, I would invite him over to the house to meet over food, coffee, or whatever—some type of meeting, the interview. That's all that remains firm. Where and how this happens is of far less importance.

Prior to the actual interview, Blake was given one or two questions that he was permitted to ask personally, or if there was a scheduling issue, I would ask on his behalf, letting the young man know that it came from Blake. Generally, because Blake knew exactly what I was interested in getting answers to, he typically asked questions that aimed at discovering what this guy (if it worked out and Claire and he started dating) liked to do that may be in common or similar to his own interests or those of our family. I have always appreciated the thought process that Blake applied during those instances. In his quintessentially empathetic nature, he was interested in knowing what the young man might like to do and experience with him and our family if things progressed beyond that *one* date.

Wherever the meeting for the interview would occur, I'd greet him with a firm, not crushing, handshake (that's too obvious), and he would return with a (hopefully) firm handshake—although his hand would be noticeably sweaty (good sign). We would sit together, face-to-face, and get the pleasantries out of the way, moving on to discuss more substantial topics. What those are is your call. This is *your* daughter and *your* interview. For me, as a Christian father, I wanted to understand more about his faith, his family, and his concept of dating.

Here's an interesting fact: when you ask a young man what his concept of dating is, he will generally give you a direct, wholesome, and succinct definition.

Paradoxically, it will likely be *exactly* what you want to hear and what he *should* say to any father. It will probably be good stuff about self-respect and respecting the girl, the parents, and the schedules and curfews, as well as more goodies like driving safely, protecting the girl, and separating himself and your daughter from unsavory influences. That's all really good because he is leading you into the next phase of your interview: your expectations. He wouldn't know it, but he would have written the opening monologue to your expectations and accountability message. Get it? He would do it to himself by deducing and then creating expectations. Celebrate that agreement. He'll think it is over, but it won't be.

Looking him directly in the eyes, I would tell him how pleased I am that he demonstrates a high level of maturity for his age and that it saves both of us a lot of time wondering what the other person is thinking and expecting. (By the way, he should *never* know what you are thinking—only what you expect.) Further, this moves him into the best part. (Make sure to tell him this is the "best part"). In a matter of seconds, I would just take him slightly off guard with the agreement and maturity compliment. Then I am about to give him the core, singular message of the interview. This must be done while he is respectfully attentive and ready to please.

I would begin to share with him how our family might be different from some he may have come to know these days. I would tell him how close we are, how much we love and care for each other, and how deeply we respect each other. I include direct and pointed comments that let him know that I am willing to do anything for my daughter to protect her—including "going back to prison!" I'm dead serious. That one always works, and it is fun for them, too, after they realize it is a joke (yet it still keeps some of his head space reserved for what you *would* do). The key here is to outline the basic expectations you have for him (whatever those are) and what methods you have to ensure accountability. Make it your own, but make it clear to him. Afterward, tell your daughter what those same expectations are (if you have not done so already).

I know some of you are thinking, if not scoffing, "This would never happen in real life!" I assure you that this *did* happen in real life, in real time, and in real direct terms with every suitor. It was one of the filters we (Claire and I) used, and it worked. She dated fine young men—without exception. I liked them and enjoyed spending time with them and their families.

It comes down to this: If your daughter is precious to you, this *is* (in your own way, of course) something you will do. If your daughter is not such a precious gift that you are willing to break away from society's norms, declare certain practices and trends morally corrupt and unwelcome in her life, and more, then you won't. Simple as that. You will set this section of the book aside, and move on to easier things. Resist that, Dad! She needs you and wants you to be the protective (not crazy or dangerous) father that God made you to be. She might even voice disagreement with some parts, but deep inside, she will be honored, grateful, and secure within a program that you have outlined for her mental, emotional, and physical health and safety. Be the dad.

When you've completed your interview, don't end abruptly. Tell him that you need to get rolling, but you don't want to leave before you are able to understand his academic and career goals. I'm not kidding; I'm serious. It is not unusual for a young man to have goals, aspirations, and perhaps clearly defined career goals in mind—I know I did. You should want to know if he does—and *if* he does, what they are. If he doesn't, fall back to his academics. Either way, you will learn more about his intelligence, his initiative, his goals, and his general outlook on life. That line of discussion is great for loosening the mood and closing the time together, and it will give you some easy and casual talking points when you see him again.

So you've read some very serious and not-so-serious things in this segment. Was it informative and fun? I hope so. If it is not both, you should take more time with this so that it is dialed in when you unveil it at home. Take what you've read, and make it your own. It can all be modified to fit your requirements or emphasis along the lines of trust, protection, and the like. If you don't know exactly what to do in one area or another, ask your wife or your friends who have gone through this—even if they didn't interview and set expectations for the prospective date. Create the standard that she will expect her date to adhere to and one that you will lead with from the beginning. Be the leader. She and her "friend" will follow.

WHEN YOU'RE NOT THERE

So what about when your daughter does not live with you, is away from home, is at college, is in the workforce, or is drifting through the single life? I hear you. This is when it gets creative and when you must step back to allow more of your daughter's strength and character to shine through. You are not there; deal with that. Rely on who you have created, nurtured, and protected to stand (almost) on her own and find her own voice and resolve.

Having said that, I must admit that it pleased me, while Claire was home from college on her first fall break, to hear her talking with Blake about the dating scene at school. He kidded her a bit, saying, "So when a guy asks you out, are you going to tell him you can't go out with him until your dad and brother interview him?"

She replied quickly and resolutely, "Of course not, but I think it will be important to have him meet Dad—and you—if we decide to take it to the boyfriend-and-girlfriend stage. I want to know that you guys approve. I am sure you will."

That was rewarding to hear. She was growing in strength and was independent enough to work these things out on her own, yet she still wanted her dad's (and brother's) input. How comforting.

Chapter 8 Recap and Checklist

- ☐ Dating is the locked-and-loaded time for fathers. Make the most of this phase in her life and yours. Be the physical and psychological impediment to folly and nefarious activity, but don't lose track of your other roles during this unique and special season of your daughter's life.
- ☐ Interview and communicate the standards you have for your daughter and what you expect from her date in the dating process. Respect is a two-way street. He must display respect to you, your daughter, and for himself in order to earn your trust and respect.
- ☐ When she leaves for college, and you're not there, you must rely on all that you have taught her. You have created, nurtured, and protected her; let her stand on her own. Let her strength and character shine through.

Maturing into a Young Woman:
Allow Her to Grow

What life stage are you at right now? Are you an expectant father? Are you playing with your toddler? Are you driving your preteen to school, sports, games, and other events? Are you worrying over your teenager who has just started to drive? Are you writing checks for your college student's tuition? Where are you? Where have you been? Where are you going? What do you do now? The answer to every life-stage question with your daughter is this: nurture her, and allow her to grow.

When you plant a new tree, you dig deep, turn up, amend, and water the soil in preparation for the tree to be planted. A good check of the root structure and being careful to guide the root base in the right direction is necessary to avoid future problems when the tree grows. You wisely place the tree, adjusting it and confirming its placement and level-straight position. Before the final watering, you'll drive a support post or two into the ground next to it and tie it with care so that when the fierce winds or driving rains come, the fragile tree will stand straight, remain in place, and grow in strength. Without the support, you know it is a matter of time before wind, rain, storm, or soil will fail your delicate sapling, and its health—or its very life—will hang in the balance.

In that analogy, you may assume correctly that I am referring, in fact, to your daughter. You and your wife have done what you can (hopefully everything you can) to dig deep, turn up, amend, and water the soil—the life experience—she has been raised in so that she can grow deep and healthy roots. You have guided her root base—her core beliefs and soul—in the right direction so that she can avoid some of the tragedies and travails of life along the way. You have stood firmly; been tied to her along with your wife (when there are two "support posts"); and held her in strength and purpose when the winds, rains, or stormy days and nights battered against her with fury.

But just as each phase of her life comes to a close, it brings with it a new one. This *next* phase requires that you remove the firmly held supports. Without the removal of the supports, a tree will fail to completely grow in strength. So will your daughter. A tree will lack the initiative to grow even deeper and stronger roots. So will your daughter. Without the removal of the firm supports, the tree may grow into and around the supports themselves, creating a tumorous bond that cannot be cut away or separated from without risk of damage or exposing a deep wound or deformation, possibly killing the tree. This is the same sad outcome your daughter will face without the strategic and loving removal of the firm supports.

Do you feel like an arborist yet? You should. It should be your life's goal to prepare, plant, care for, and then allow to grow freely a tree—a resilient and loving daughter—that will grow deeper and deeper roots. Her canopy of sturdy branches will stretch out boldly over a lost and dying world, providing shade and comfort to many who would be drawn to her beauty, strength, and purpose, knowing it all came from deep, well-watered roots and a solid core within.

I've seen plenty of the opposite. We all have. It is a sad sight, painful to behold, and a heartbreaking tragedy to experience when it reveals itself within the bounds of friendship or family. Those types of trees parasitically cling to the host—whether parents, friends, family, or society. They have only learned to receive, to take, and to expect from others. They can be entitled and immature at their core, becoming society's burden, the modern-day "snowflake," confused, or chemically dependent (or worse).

At whatever life stage you find yourself today, take hold of the parallel that exists with your daughter and her growth and eventual departure into life. Let her go. Let her *grow*.

SEND HER INTO THE WORLD WITH "LETTERS OF LOVE"

Think back to chapter 2 when we talked about the letters of love, encouragement, hopes, and dreams. Do you have something like that? Have you documented stages of your daughter's life or your hopes and dreams for her? Maybe it's video messages. Perhaps it is poetry or a photo collage. I don't know what you could do that fits for your relationship and life journey, but I do know that you *should* do something. Figure out what you can do now at whatever stage you find yourself in.

A great time to share the letters (for example) would be when she graduates from college, gets married, or takes some other similarly significant, next-level step in her life. So, whatever that "something" is, nail down a time to present it to her. Send her into the world with a measured gift that represents your love and confidence in her. Support her growth and purpose in this world by committing tokens of the *past* to a woman taking on her *future*. It will be great. You both will never forget it.

SHARING TOUGH STUFF—A BOND THAT BRINGS YOU AND YOUR MATURE DAUGHTER CLOSER

I don't expect that this is going to be the most uplifting segment you'll read, but it is important. There are a few bonds that bring you and your mature daughter closer than experiencing and sharing the tough stuff we all face from time to time in life. I am not suggesting you unduly burden or chain your daughter down to problematic or trying situations and circumstances. That could be harmful. But keeping them from her may also be detrimental in the long run.

Here is how I separate the two. Tragedies are events that take place, in most cases, outside of our control and often without satisfactory resolution. The death of a loved one, a serious illness, and difficult relational issues that would directly affect you or your daughter are all subjects that should be shared and discussed with her. Your shattered dreams (career, personal, relational, etc.) and other serious but clearly secondary matters as they relate to your daughter should only be shared and discussed as a "for instance," "for example," and "for comparison" when you are already engaged in a situation or discussion about a directly correlated issue she is dealing with and needs real-world advice, council, and prayer. Our kids can learn from our mistakes, tragedies that befall us, and even our broken dreams. However, don't ever allow pity, ego, or an agenda to get in the way of the life lesson that you are presenting to her.

DARK SUBJECTS

Perhaps, depending upon your age or the age of your parents, you may not have been raised in an open or conversational family environment. Some families do not discuss hard topics or share dark subject matter—ever. I understand that. I do not condone or agree with it, but I understand it.

I grew up in a family that was led by parents who both came from broken homes and who both knew tragedy early in life. For my dad, before he escaped his teen years, he would be emotionally and mentally scarred by his experiences in World War II in the Pacific—the kind of experiences that would shatter the fragile story line of existing blockbuster movies of World War II and capture the essence and irrevocable pain and suffering of our brave solders in the Pacific. These were part of his life.

Deployed into the heart of the Pacific battles and amid hundreds of islands and many thousands of dead and wounded, my father served in the US Navy (Go Navy! Beat Army!) aboard the hospital ship USS *Solace*. He worked as a Pharmacist's Mate First Class and a part-time ship's photographer, and he sometimes found himself attached to marine units throughout the theater as a medical corpsman of sorts. There was guard duty and a lot of hard work to do back then too. It was war, so you did whatever you were asked to do.

As I write this, my father is ninety-two years old. In the seventy-five years that have passed since his enlistment, I have heard only a few hard stories. They are difficult to hear, imagine, and contemplate – let alone experience first-hand as he did. Sure, I have heard the fun stories—the stories of comradery and lighthearted fun—but there are more hard stories that rarely come to the top.

The hard stories and dark realities of war are difficult to voice—nearly crippling for my father—so most of them they lie undisturbed beneath layers of memories, nightmares, and anxiety that have weighed him down for seventy-five years. These are wounds that do not heal on their own. An enlightened society knows that now. These psychological gashes are grotesque, unsightly open wounds that ooze and bleed. But you'd never know because they are meticulously bandaged, bound, wrapped, and hidden away from others. That is the way his generation addressed posttraumatic stress issues and the like.

These recollections of war, death, and unspeakable atrocities by a heartless enemy are retained by a man who was arguably just a boy when deployed. Though my father returned from war to become a medical doctor, a renowned surgeon, and a professor, he was not able to do more for himself or in the name of healing than to bind, bandage, and hide the wounds of war for a lifetime.

I contend that if my father had shared more with those who love, care, and protect him, he could have been so much further along (though any promise of complete healing is so rarely realized in this life). I wish my father could have found a way to limit his attachment to the past and welcomed the future, instead of limiting his connections with people, friends, and family.

You will find no judgment in my words—only sadness, pity, and vicarious regret. Like so many of his generation, he is a hero, a patriot, and deserving of so much more from each of us in this country. Like many, he was a selfless citizen warrior who did not ask for the fight but was proud to be a part of ending it.

When I consider the so-called "snowflakes" of this present generation, I reflect on my father, my grandfather, and the other men in my family (going back to the War of Independence) and the millions of heroic men and women who have preserved our great country, defended our freedom, and sought to bring peace out from the sin of war. There is no comparison. There is no deliberation required. Men like my father come from a remarkable generation that we see only a glimpse of today. The selfish, entitled anarchists of this present age could not hold a candle—or their five-dollar café latte—to men like my father and patriots like him.

With dark subjects come hard realities. Be sure to remember those in your life who may *not* share but need your strength just as much as those who *do*. Reach out to them.

LET THE WOUNDS BREATHE

Medically speaking, have you noticed that something as simple as a cut or abrasion—not to mention a severe wound—will not heal if it remains bandaged? Have you considered that no level of care, cutting-edge medication, or antibiotics applied to it will affect a complete healing without uncovering it? Wounds must eventually breathe. Wounds must eventually see the light of day. They will not heal without airing out.

Like a physical wound, the wounds we all have in this life must be aired out in the healing process. As adults, when we progress through a healing process, after we've prayed and done all we can internally, we may need to "air it out" or "let it breathe." This may occur in the presence of our spouse, a dear friend, a pastor, or someone else you trust implicitly. Those confidants are all good. They can all promote the longer term healing process. What about your children? In this case, what about your daughter?

While I do not ascribe to the concept of parenting from the perspective of a contemporary friend, I do see value in sharing the dark realities of life. I believe it is entirely possible to be the leader, the parent, and the respected authority figure in your daughter's life as well as being free to share the deeper thoughts, challenges, and pains of life. The only caveat I would place on that would be to do it when you *are* in process, in control, or in reflection of an event or problem.

In my estimation, it would be an emotionally dangerous situation (for both of you) when and if you shared an open and bleeding wound with your daughter that is a "secondary matter"—something that is not of vital need or importance to know—without the benefit of completion. In other words, if it is a secondary matter, you should be in the final stages of processing it yourself, in complete control of the realities, or sharing in reflection (looking back) on the subject in order to aid your daughter in an area of her own life or circumstance.

The risk of sharing things that could be sad, embarrassing, or melancholy could, in fact, prevent even deeper issues in your daughter's life. By taking an emotional risk yourself and conveying a dark, depressing, or painful struggle that you overcame (or have obtained specific and useful perspective from) can help her in many ways.

Your daughter is mature now. She knows you are not perfect. She knows that you *are* real. When you prove both of these points by sharing hard things, you prevent or cure the isolation that could come in her path if she thinks she is not understood or that she alone fights a specific battle within herself or in the circumstance she finds herself in.

SHE STILL NEEDS YOUR INPUT, YOUR LOVE, AND YOUR RESPECT
CAREER

Statistically speaking, your daughter will enter a profession after college or trade school. This first step toward a career will likely be one of a few professional steps she'll take (up and down) over her many years in the workforce. When she jumps in and focuses on it like a career and not a job, she will have highs and lows, experience unfair and uncomplimentary attitudes, and live in realities that she may find uncommon to her own life experiences. When this happens, she will communicate those trials. If your relationship is what you expect it will be, you will be on the list of people she confides in. When that moment comes, be the dad.

It would be easy for you, in your own desire to remain connected to her, to be the "support post" by engaging in what some may term as *office gossip* or *loose chatter*. Avoid that at all costs (and hopefully she will too). Limit your career talk to acting as a sounding board when necessary and a mature voice of reason and expectation as you encourage her to stand strong on her own. "Here is what is reasonable…" and "Here is what you can and should expect…" are the lines you should be on. Good advice to her should be limited to topics that she simply could not perceive or steer through without the benefit of the thirty or more years of career experience that you have. Give her insight. Give her tools to deal with disappointments in the office, but don't engage in the petty. You and your experience are bigger than that. Show her respect by being professional and expecting the same from her. She deserves that.

RELATIONSHIPS

Depending upon the type and tenor of your relationship with your daughter before she left home to be on her own—and the type and tenor of your relationship with your wife—your daughter may or may not contact you regarding relationship issues. If she doesn't, then don't push, pry, or manipulate family time or your limited phone, e-mail, or other connection points you have together to question, inquire, or check on her.

If she does contact, share, or ask for your help with regard to a relationship issue, be grateful, be respectful, and be loving. Don't be surprised if the "issue" stems from a specific warning, a "no-go zone," or other boundary you set in place years ago. Don't be surprised if your perfect little angel has crossed over a few lines and moved a few boundary markers you've set over time and then realized they were there for a reason.

Whatever her relational situation, remember that she is on her own now. She is an adult. She is completely responsible for the situation—and likely the outcome as well. Give her the rope to tie herself off to something more secure. Give her the rope to help *her* pull *herself* back up from the cliff. Give her the rope, the connection, and the security that you are there. Don't give her the proverbial rope with which to hang herself over the situation to somehow show you were right. Love her through the pain and frustration and show her the way toward the solution, but don't *be* the solution. She needs to work that out on her own. That's the only way she'll grow tall and stretch out those branches.

DISAPPOINTMENTS

There is a saying that goes something like this: "Life is full of disappointments. Get over it." Ouch! Whoever said that was correct, but isn't there a better way to say it? The truth is that sometimes there is no better way to convey the message. Life is, in fact, full of disappointments. Careers, expectations, dreams, goals, sickness, family, relationships, and love lost are only a few aspects of life to feel discontent or disenchanted over. But there is more to this otherwise melancholy story line.

Those same areas of dissatisfaction also, coincidently, may run concurrently to and hold the greatest capacity for contentment, joy, and pleasure. Have you ever been disappointed in a given situation, but once you considered it for yourself or were pointed to the other areas of your life that are not so "disappointing," you actually got over it? We all have. When disappointments come her way, gently (and with great respect and deference to her feelings at the moment) be the voice (not the reminding nag) that points her to the other areas of her life.

TRAGEDIES

Tragedies will befall each of us in due time. It hurts, but it is a very rare life indeed that cannot recount tragedy. Like you, I am familiar with seemingly "perfect" people with "perfect lives" who live with no apparent tragedies in the areas of family, relationship, love, career, income, dreams, health, or anything else. There is one problem with that thought: that person and family do not exist. If you know people who seem like that, you simply don't know them well enough. Peel back the onion, and something there will make you cry.

I once held someone in very high regard for a time in my life and career. He had an enviable career, a great home and pool, and income to spare, and he traveled to many of the places I would have liked to have gone. I once considered why my life, career, and income was not similar to his. It's funny how easily we peer over the fence at the greener grass on the other side, yet we remember with difficulty that the grass is greenest where it is *watered*.

It turns out that he was watering his career, his perks, his travel, and his income potential, while failing to water his family. Within a few years of meeting him, becoming friends, and wondering why the life he had was not my own, his life collapsed around him. He lost his job, nearly lost his second marriage, and two of his kids were doing (not experimenting with) drugs in their junior-high and high-school years (one of them requiring residential treatment that cost nearly $40,000 out of pocket). He changed a lot about his life after that.

Some ten years later, he and I reconnected at an industry event. He said something that broke me to the core. He told me he wanted to share something personal, asking if it was okay. I said yes, assuring him that friends do that with friends. He said, "I wanted you to know that, for years, I had the life I wanted—the career I chose and the money to spend on vacations, the home, the pool, and more. In the end, I figured out that all I *really* needed was what *you* have—a family, a good job, and a wife and kids who love you. Keep it up, buddy. You have it all."

I will never forget that conversation. Neither should you.

Tragedies come in all shapes and sizes. Make sure your love, respect, and listening ear are tuned to her tragedies and those around her so that you can be a voice of reason and a reality check when necessary.

SUICIDE

Don't skip out on me now, men. You need to hear this. Suicide rates are on the rise in the United States and around the world. Why? Who? What can be done? These are all questions to be addressed by professionals in the mental-health community. What you and I need to know is that the female rates of suicide are increasing appreciably.

The incidents of suicide by women have not surpassed men, but there are other reasons for that too. Put bluntly, men typically succeed when they choose suicide, while women often fail. That statistic is changing. In the end, it is an epidemic that few are discussing. Poor body image, self-loathing, imperfection, or rejection within a world order that says women should act like men and men like women—all are certainly a part of it.

The data compiled from sixty-three countries shows a correlation with the unemployment crisis. Why?

I wonder if it has anything to do with a world that tells her she has to be perfect and have it all. Or is it our modern society that demands that every woman have a career or she is worthless? Or is it when the career she trains and goes to college for is not there for her, or she is summarily fired when the "latest model" arrives off the college floor? This may lead her to become distraught and seek a permanent solution.

I am not a mental-health professional, but I am a father and a man who believes that women in America and around the world have been sold a rotten apple. For you and me, we need the comprehensive approach to this at a micro level—a home level.

Our daughters need to be raised to understand the principles of a life well lived. They need to know that a career on the way to or during the family years does not define who they are. They need to know that they might actually be better off—as would some of their kids—if they worked from home or walked away from the career world for a few years while they raised their children. This may take compromise and strategy on the part of the husband too, but bridging the gap and addressing these realities is a worthy endeavor for any woman, any husband, and any family.

Our daughters need to learn from a young age that family comes before career and that self-esteem is not tied to the mirror, the boardroom, or any other misdirected craft of the media, women's magazines, or the like. No matter what the world tells her, she has eternal worth just the way she was created. Remind her of that. Raise her with love and respect while helping her to avoid the polytheistic world of "women's rights" that can actually hold her back. Remind her that the world is better off with her in it.

HOPE

Men, we need to instill hope in the hearts of our daughters. It will not come naturally for most of us, but we need to make a determined effort.

We need to show her that faith and hope are real, and in Christ, we have hope in the midst of a hopeless world.

We need to demonstrate hope by aspiring to make the world a better place. This happens by recognizing evil that exists and exhibits itself around the world daily—and by reaching out to others in big and small ways. Demonstrating hope to her at a young age will ensure she will embody that same spirit for change and improvement when she grows up. When your daughter sees that little things can change big problems and that hope can alter what would otherwise be an insurmountable situation, she will hold fast and be the leader to those around her in their time of need.

When the world looks hopeless to her along life's journey, she will know in her heart and head that there is always hope, always a way, and always a Savior to rely on and place *her* hope in. "Praise be to the God and Father of our Lord Jesus Christ! In his great mercy he has given us new birth into a living hope through the resurrection of Jesus Christ from the dead" (1 Pet. 1:3).

Chapter 9 Recap and Checklist

☐ Allow her to grow. You have provided for her, protected her, and shown her the way. Now let her walk her life's path.

☐ Send her into the world with letters of love or whatever you have organized that documented your hopes, dreams, and love for her through the various stages of her life.

☐ Sharing the tough stuff is a bond that will bring you and your *mature* daughter closer. She will experience hard things in life; let her know they can be overcome. Dark subjects must be allowed to breathe at some point in life. Help her understand that even with dark topics, there can be growth and healing in the release. Be that example.

☐ She will still need your input, your love, and your respect as she moves into the career world, into relationships, and through disappointments and tragedies. Be there for her in every area she invites you into. Show her respect as you provide needed wisdom. Be Dad.

☐ Female suicide rates are increasing. Remind her that family comes before career and that self-esteem is not tied to the mirror, the boardroom, or any other misdirected craft of the media, women's magazines, or anything else the world tells her.

☐ Instill hope in the heart of your daughter. Do it today; whatever her age, instill hope. Show her that faith and hope are real, and in Christ, we have hope in the midst of a hopeless world. Demonstrate hope by aspiring to make the world a better place. There is always hope, always a way, and always a Savior to rely on and place *her* hope in.

10

What Remains: Final Thoughts for You, Dad

You may come to this, the final chapter, and carry some level of discontentment, insecurity, or even disagreement with something you have read in the preceding pages. If so, I invite you to discard or embrace all that you have read with this in mind: I wrote this for you.

With sincerity and great humility, I have confessed and demonstrated to you that I am imperfect, I am flawed, and I have failed any number of times and ways along this parenting journey. However, I never gave up.

There is no guilt or blame to bear as you read and recall the elements of this book. If you have not been the dad you should have been up to this point, change. If you get busy right now, from the point you are at, and endeavor to be the dad your daughter needs, you will be doing the right thing. If time has passed you and your daughter by, and you recognize your failings, that is hard, I know, but it is healthy. Now—right now—do something positive with that. Don't just roll over and call it done. Never give up.

NO APOLOGIES

When I sat down in my office to write this book, I did not focus on creating a Christian book on parenting. I felt then—and I still do—that parenting your daughter and earning the title of "Dad" are not distinctly Christian issues.

If you are not a follower of Christ, and you still stuck with this book but did not appreciate the inserted references, scriptures, or quotes from our Savior, I cannot help but think there is a reason for that. I cannot apologize for it because for me separating parenting from my faith and all that Jesus has done for me is an impossibility. I could no more separate God's work and His will in my life (and within the parenting process) than I could oxygen from my lungs—so I didn't try.

Through the preceding chapters, you read what I wrote as I shared from the heart. Along the way, you have read about Jesus, the Son of God, who came to earth to rescue you from sin and join you in heaven when your time on earth is complete.

If you don't know Him, I invite you to introduce yourself today, and you'll find out that He knew you before time began. He knows your name. Tell Him you know you are a sinner and that you know He is the one true God. Tell Him you believe that He came to save your soul. Ask him to forgive you of all your sins and cleanse you today. That is it. That is the beginning of an eternal journey. I pray that I meet you someday as a new man in Christ. You'll be a new father to your daughter—at whatever stage you find yourself in—and the new man God intended for you to be all along.

INTO THE FIRE

Those who know me recognize that I am an unrepentant music addict who owns hundreds of CDs by many artists and spanning many genres. I am a lover of music with its beat, tempo, lyrics, and the gentle or rough touch it has on people. It is one of my passions. In fact, one of my many secret dreams since childhood was to be a recording artist. If I could today, I would. Alas, that is not the life I lead. So, I remain a legend in my car, my office, and anywhere else I can sing freely.

Music is something that simply cannot be removed from my life. Without music, this world would be (without sounding too melodramatic) a silent scream inside the nightmare that doesn't end, a thunderless summer storm, or (at best) quite boring.

As I considered this closing chapter, I wondered to myself, "What song would capture the sense of duty, honor, and warrior mode that you should feel as a father of a daughter? What lyrics could possibly illustrate the awe-inspiring responsibility you have when you earn the title of 'Dad'? What could describe the incredibly heroic challenges that lie before you on your way toward earning the title?" I came to one conclusion: "Into the Fire." It's an epic refrain written by Nan Knighton and Frank Wildhorn and is performed on the album *Stand Ye Steady: Songs of Courage and Inspiration*, performed by Daniel Rodriguez and the USMA Cadet Glee Club.

With my strongest recommendation, considering all that you have read, buy the CD, song, or DVD or watch the video on YouTube. I offer what I know of the lyrics below, but do not rely on them alone. Read it as you listen to it being sung. Remember, as fathers, we are all called into battle—valleys, mountains, waters, dangers, storms, and (for some) the proverbial hell. Let that song—the words, the tempo, and crescendos—move you. Don't hesitate to rush in for your daughter. Do not think for a moment that she won't be worth the costs or any cost. Into the fire we go!

Into the Fire
David walked into the valley
With a stone clutched in his hand
He was only a boy,
But he knew someone must take a stand

There will always be a valley
Always mountains one must scale
There will always be perilous waters
Which someone must sail

Into valleys, into waters
Into jungles, into hell
Let us ride, let us ride home again with a story to tell
Into darkness, into danger
Into storms that rip the night

Don't give in, don't give up
But give thanks for the glorious fight

You can tremble, you can fear it
But keep your fighting spirit alive, boys
Let the shiver of it sting you
Fling into battle, spring to your feet, boys
Never hold back your step for a moment
Never doubt that your courage will grow
Hold your head even higher and into the fire we go

Are there mountains that surround us?
Are there walls that block the way?
Knock 'em down, strip 'em back, boys
And forward and into the fray

Into terror, into valor
Charge ahead, no, never turn
Yes, it's into the fire we fly
And the devil will burn

Someone has to face the valley
Rush in, we have to rally and win, boys
When the world is saying not to
By God, you know you've got to march on, boys
Never hold back your step for a moment
Never doubt that your courage will grow
Hold your head ever higher and into the fire we go

Let the lightning strike
Let the force of it shock you
Choke your fears away
Pull as tight as a wire

Let the fever strike
Let the force of it rock you
We will have our day, sailing into the fire

Someone has to face the valley
Rush in! We have to rally and win, boys
When the world is saying not to
By God, you know you've got to march on, boys
Never hold back your step for a moment
Look alive! Oh, your courage will grow
Hold your head ever higher and into the fire we go!

—Nan Knighton and Frank Wildhorn

THOUGHTS, REMINDERS, AND CHALLENGES

I leave you with the following thoughts, reminders, and challenges. Take them to heart. Earn the title of "Dad." Earn it in your own special way (not *necessarily* in the way I did) and *hold fast*! Never give up!

- ✓ There is no perfect home; nor is there a perfect dad. You and I are both rock-solid proof of that fact. The risk to you is minimal, and the reward for you both is so great. Don't leave this book, your daughter, your family, or this world with any regrets. Be the dad!
- ✓ Maybe this book has brought you back to a dark place deep within the recesses of your childhood—a segment of your life that you locked away years ago, yet the fear, pain, and memories haunt you. If that describes you and your childhood, prevent her from knowing that for herself. Make her childhood different, special, and memorable.
- ✓ If you weren't protected, protect her. If you didn't have the dad you needed, be the dad *she* needs. Don't allow whatever occurred in your past to rob you of your future with your daughter—and especially her God-given future with *her* dad.
- ✓ If you feel like you are drawing from an empty well, fill up on the Word of God. The Bible is the best parenting book ever written, a best seller worth reading. Get busy becoming what *you* have always wanted and hoped for. She deserves all that you hope, dream, and pray for her.
- ✓ Remember that giving her a better life than what you had does not mean "things." It means time, love, devotion, care, support, and more.
- ✓ You are Dad for a lifetime. No matter what her age, she will always need some part of you—your input, your love, and your respect. Remember to always be available, Dad. Give her your time.
- ✓ Listen. Use what you've been given (two ears); learn from your daughter; and see her life through her eyes, experiences, and heart.

Be patient. Invest the time. When you're not patient, you're not listening *or* learning.

✓ Claire is one of my best friends. I am grateful for that relationship. It is wonderful to be in a close relationship and friendship with your daughter or your son; however, never confuse or get tangled up in what should be clearly defined lines between friendship and fatherhood. You are a father first and foremost. Friendship is a sweet by-product of parenting well—never the opposite.

✓ Wisdom. Get it, strive after it, pray for it, and educate yourself in the lost art of listening to learn. When it comes to your daughter, you will learn from her, but you'll need to be there. You will need to listen.

✓ Expectations. We live in a world of unrealistic expectations. Do not allow the ludicrous expectations of this world, our society, or your own self-directed ego to guide your daughter. She does not need to emulate a pop star, an actress, or a first lady. She needs to be *herself—her* best.

What would America—or the world—look like today if every daughter were raised by parents who simply *expected* the best instead of something else? How much more advanced we would be as a society if daughters were *expected* to simply be kind-natured, respectful, giving citizens, who loved their families and their communities and who had a moral compass to follow? We would be surrounded by women of strength, honor, and purpose who cared more for others than for the waning fame of social status or social media.

Our goal for our daughters should be that they grow to be strong, faithful women who measure their success by the grace they show, the people they help along the way, and the lasting imprint they leave on this world when they are gone. Raise them to be world changers.

✓ Final instructions: King David, in the Old Testament, said to his son Solomon, "Now devote your heart and soul to seeking the Lord your God" (I Chron. 22:13b).

There can be no better final instruction—not from me, but from *you*—to your children. When you teach your daughter, teach her to devote herself and her very heart and soul to seek after the Lord God. It is the only lasting instruction you should concern yourself with. Everything else is secondary.

FORGET THE T-SHIRT

On Father's Day, you've seen the T-shirts, the ties, the hats, and the bumper stickers that say, "World's Greatest Dad." If you are reaching for that title and feeling like you've come up short, there is a reason for that. You *have* come up short. You have stepped up to bat, swung hard, and missed. You have failed miserably—but *only* at the impossible.

You know, I have failed too. And I can tell you from experience why you'll never earn that title. The title *world's greatest dad* is an unattainable designation. That title is held by one alone: our Lord and Savior, the creator of the universe, your soul, and all that you will ever know into the limits of eternity. There can be no greater father on heaven or on earth—and so there *isn't*.

He stands at the door of your heart today, knocking and waiting with open arms to be *your* Heavenly Father (*your Dad*) today. If you do not know Him as *your* Dad, *your* Father, *your* Savior and King, I pray that you will accept Him into your heart today.

"Behold, I stand at the door and knock. If anyone hears my voice and opens the door, I will come in to him and eat with him, and he with me." (Revelation 3:20)

For you and your daughter, the best you and I can strive for, resolve in our hearts, and pray over to live out every day is to earn the title of "_____'s dad."

Go ahead, Dad. Take a pen and write in her beautiful name. Write your daughter's name on that line, and live the kind of life being her dad requires of you.

Be her dad today, tomorrow, and for the rest of your life!

Hold fast. Never give up.

—Shad

Afterword by Claire E. Arnold

Reading through my dad's philosophy, opinions, and advice about parenting, I found they were both familiar and eye-opening. While I had recognized the importance of Dad's actions, I had not previously had the privilege of reading into his mind-set or the principles behind his parenting motives to understand why he did certain things as my father. Each memory that he recounted in this book reminded me of what I experienced during that time as well as displayed to me his valuable point of view as an understanding father.

For years, family and friends have wondered how and why Dad and I are so close. The truth is that he always pursued my well-being, putting into action everything mentioned in this book. Consequently, I strongly believe that I have the best dad in the world. I do not claim that just because I love him. I claim it because he has been and will always be the pure definition of a father to me—a father who additionally opens himself up for "female talk," joking, crying, hugging, counseling, heroism, and friendship. He truly exemplifies the qualities God calls for in a man, father, and friend.

I cannot express how grateful I am to have been surrounded by such an involved and loving family. Being blessed with a dad who holds being a father and husband above all other earthly attractions is a dream for many daughters. Thankfully, it is reality for me.

So, in saying all of this, I hope your daughter will be able to tell you these same types of things in the future as she recognizes and embraces your ceaseless concern for her. You have the tools and love to earn the title of "Dad," one of the most honorable and respectable positions any man can hold in life. Your daughter needs you. Go fulfill your vocation.

—Claire

Made in the USA
Middletown, DE
27 May 2019